Secrets of the Proverbs 31 WOMAN

Secrets of the Proverbs 31 WOMAN

Fresh Perspectives on Biblical Wisdom for Women

Rae Simons

BARBOUR BOOKS
An Imprint of Barbour Publishing, Inc.

Print ISBN 978-1-63058-861-8

eBook Editions:
Adobe Digital Edition (.epub) 978-1-63409-280-7
Kindle and MobiPocket Edition (.prc) 978-1-63409-281-4

Published by Barbour Books, an imprint of Barbour Publishing, Inc., P.O. Box 719, Uhrichsville, Ohio 44683, www.barbourbooks.com.

Our mission is to publish and distribute inspirational products offering exceptional value and biblical encouragement to the masses.

Member of the
Evangelical Christian
Publishers Association

Printed in Canada.

Introduction

The book of Proverbs is full of word pictures that help us understand deep truths. One that recurs again and again is the comparison of wisdom to a woman. This woman is strong and outspoken; she shouts in the streets (1:20). In the long passage found in the thirty-first chapter we learn still more about her.

Verse after verse, this passage of scripture affirms our identity as women. The woman we see in Proverbs 31 is committed to her relationships; her husband and children depend on her and are blessed by her. She works hard and efficiently, with initiative and creativity. She knows how to use her skills to make money, but she also reaches out to those in need. She takes care of herself as well.

Each detail is not meant to describe a specific, single woman. In other words, we don't need to add them to our to-do lists! Instead, Proverbs 31 shows us a larger picture of what we are all capable of being as women. It's like a mirror God holds up for us to look into—and then He says, "See? This is who I created you to be."

As women, God calls us to embody love and wisdom. Each of us will do that differently, with our unique skills and individual strengths—but we all have amazing things to offer the world. We don't need to be afraid to be strong, to be wise, to try new things. God believes in us!

This is the sort of book that's intended to be read slowly, one meditation at a time. Doing so will give you time to ponder each section of this scripture and apply it to your own life. Hear what God has to say to you through the Proverbs 31 woman!

PART I

Who can find a virtuous woman?
for her price is far above rubies.
—VERSE 10 KJV

Strong, Capable, Creative

When you hear the phrase *virtuous woman*, what does it call to mind? Most of us probably think of a "good woman," someone who obeys the Bible and avoids sin. Personally, I picture a matronly woman dressed in a modest, nondescript dress, with a calm look on her face. Sadly, I don't identify with this woman because I know I fall far short of her serenity and purity. And if I'm honest—well, frankly, I find her a little boring.

As twenty-first-century women, we find it hard to reconcile our own lives with the ancient standard of excellence offered to us in Proverbs. Our culture today is so different from that which existed in the Near East, hundreds of years before Christ. Adding to our difficulty, Christian men through the centuries have held up these verses to their wives and daughters as the perfect example of what a Christian woman should be. Sometimes, as women, we may feel a little resentful at having so much "goodness" demanded of us!

Our discomfort with these verses may be caused in part, though, simply because of differences in our twenty-first-century language from that used when the King James Bible was written. If you look up the word *virtuous* in a modern dictionary, you'll find that it means "righteous, morally upright, saintly, principled, ethical." There's nothing wrong with being all those things, of course! But this definition isn't quite what the ancient author had in mind, and it wasn't what the seventeenth-century translators were shooting for either when they used the word *virtuous.* Back in the 1600s, someone who was virtuous was strong and courageous, filled with power to bring about good in the world. It was a word used to describe knights, not meek little women!

If we turn to other versions of the Bible, we find that where the King James Version uses *virtuous*, more modern translations of Proverbs offer words like *excellent, capable, diligent, noble,* and *worthy.* These words get us a little closer to what the ancient author had in mind millennia ago when he composed these verses.

The Hebrew word used here points us even more directly back to the seventeenth-century understanding of what it meant to be virtuous. The word is *chayil,* and according to Strong's Concordance, it means "strong, effective, and brave." It's a word that was used to describe armies, troops that were valiant and mighty, with plenty of resources to draw from.

Our modern-day society often considers goodness to be boring, but earlier cultures knew it was just the opposite. Good people are strong and brave; they're the people who change the world for the better; they're the people God uses to accomplish amazing things. When the ancient author of Proverbs wrote this passage, he wasn't imagining a woman who was the least bit dull!

In fact, the Bible's image of the perfect woman was pretty radical. During pre-Christian Bible times, women were generally considered to be second-rate people, inferior to men—but these verses in Proverbs offered a far different perspective. The Proverbs 31 woman was strong, capable, and creative.

These words, written thousands of years ago, still inspire and challenge us as women today. God is calling us to be like valiant knights in shining armor, riding out to bring God's justice and love to the world around us.

*Dear God, I ask that You help me to
be truly virtuous. Make me strong with
Your strength and courageous with Your
courage. Use me to do great things.*

How Will We Live?

The word *virtue* shows up throughout the Bible. When we look at how it's used in other scripture verses, we may get an even better idea of what it means to be a "virtuous woman."

In 2 Peter 1:5, Peter writes, "Giving all diligence, add to your faith virtue; and to virtue knowledge" (KJV). He's telling us that we need to support our trust in God with virtue's active goodness. In other words, our faith inspires us to take action! It gives us energy to accomplish great things, but we don't just run around doing everything we can think of; we temper our virtue with understanding and wisdom.

When the psalmist wrote, "They go from strength to strength, till each appears before God in Zion" (Psalm 84:7 NIV), the Hebrew word translated as "strength" is the same as that translated as "virtuous" in Proverbs 31, and once again, it's connected to well-supplied armies that can fight confidently and bravely. The promise here is given to all of us who "dwell in God's house": we will increase in power, in courage, and in our ability to do God's work.

In the book of Ruth, when Boaz announced to his community that he was going to marry Ruth, the elders said to him, "May the LORD make the woman who is coming into your home like Rachel and Leah, both of whom built the house of Israel; and may you achieve wealth in Ephrathah" (4:11 NASB). In this verse, the Hebrew word translated "wealth" is *chayil*, the same word used for "virtue" in Proverbs 31. The Jewish elders were comparing Ruth, a woman from Moab, to Rachel and Leah, two of the great women of the Old Testament whose energy and courage helped make Israel a strong nation.

So what does that mean to us today as women? If we are virtuous women, how will we live? How will we think of ourselves?

Lord of my life, I ask that You help me to see myself with Your eyes. May I see the strong woman You have called to serve You. Wipe away my self-doubt. Heal my sense that I'm not good enough, talented enough, smart enough, or capable enough. I believe in You, Lord, and I ask You now to add energy and courage to my belief. I put myself in Your hands, trusting that You will lead me from strength to strength. Make me like Ruth, like Rachel and Leah. Use me to build Your house.

Women Of Virtue

When the ancient author sat down to write these verses in Proverbs, I wonder if he had a real woman in mind, someone he knew. Was it his own wife who inspired him to write these words? Or his mother? Did he realize that the world is full of women of strength and courage, women with an active faith in God who work hard to make the world a better place for all of us?

When I look at my own experience, I see how women of virtue have shaped my life. I think of my mother reading to me every night before I went to bed, even when she was falling asleep herself after a long day of work. I think of my mother-in-law who always welcomed us to a house that was filled with the scent of fresh-made tomato sauce. I think of my grandmothers, each with her own brand of resolute courage in the face of hardship. I think of my friends and sisters, women who have known me all my life, who love me and forgive me and understand me, year after year. I think of my teachers and mentors, women who showed me how to grow, how to go further and climb higher, both professionally and spiritually.

We all have women like these in our lives. And when we look at history, we see other women of virtue, a long chain of women that spans the centuries. The great women of the Old Testament—Sarah, Esther, and Deborah, for example—give us examples of women who were neither meek nor boring; instead, they were strong-minded, active women who stood up courageously for their people. If we shift our attention to more recent history, women like Harriet Beecher Stowe and Florence Nightingale once again proved that courageous women could change the world for the better. Harriet Beecher Stowe's book, *Uncle Tom's Cabin*, so powerfully influenced readers' minds that it helped to bring about the end of slavery in the United States, while Florence Nightingale improved soldiers' wartime medical treatment as she also opened up the field of nursing to women. In the twentieth century, Rosa Parks's courage sparked the civil rights movement, and Mother Teresa's devotion to the poor inspired the world to do more for those in need. All of these women lived lives of faith and commitment, giving all of their strength to serve God and others.

Today, we can be both challenged and encouraged by the women of virtue who have gone before us. From our perspective, these women may seem like extraordinary heroines—but from their own, they were just ordinary women who got up each morning and did ordinary things with love and commitment. Doing those "ordinary things" over and over and over sometimes takes the most courage and strength of all—and those seemingly small things are often what God uses to change the world.

Dear God, I thank You for the women of virtue who have gone before me. Thank You for all the ways You used them to bring Your love to me and to the world. May I be inspired by their examples. Use me, I pray, as You used them. May I, too, work courageously for Your kingdom. I give myself to You, Lord.

Treasures Within

According to the author of Proverbs, the price of a virtuous woman "is far above rubies" (KJV). At first glance, I'm not sure I like the idea that a woman has a price, even if it's a high one. Women aren't chattel, after all; we can't be bought and sold. But when I look again, I realize that is exactly what the scripture is saying: no price whatsoever can be put on the virtuous woman because she is not something that can be purchased. In fact, she is more valuable than any material wealth.

Besides a virtuous woman, there's only one other thing in the Bible that's said to be more valuable than rubies—wisdom. Proverbs 3:15 tells us that wisdom is "more precious than rubies; nothing you desire can compare with her" (NIV). Job 28:18 says that "the price of wisdom is above rubies" (KJV), and we read in Proverbs 20:15 that "wise words are more valuable than. . .rubies" (NLT). By implication then, Proverbs 31 is comparing a virtuous woman to wisdom. That's quite a compliment!

Wisdom is more than intelligence, and it's far deeper than mere knowledge. Wisdom is one of God's own attributes. According to the Bible, the wise person doesn't just follow all the rules but instead acts, thinks, and lives in total harmony with God's will.

Wisdom is another aspect of a Proverbs 31 woman's virtue. A woman of virtue lives in harmony with God, and that harmony spreads out through her life. As a result, she also lives in harmony with other people. Wisdom leads her to act in ways that bring peace between herself and those around her, and wisdom also brings her into harmony with herself. As she allows herself to be caught up in God's will, she finds a sense of self-worth and inner peace. She knows her value comes from God.

Aristotle said, "Knowing yourself is the beginning of wisdom." When we start to get to know ourselves, we will also get to know God—and when we get to know God, we will also understand our own selves better. It works both ways.

This is the source of our wisdom as women: we are on a journey of discovery with God. He is pointing out in us the things He values; He is revealing places where we can grow; and He is leading us into an adventure that will last our entire lifetimes—and continue on even after this life. Who knows what treasures we will discover within God and within our own hearts along the way?

Dear Lord, thank You that You treasure me. Help me to know my true worth in Your eyes. Teach me to follow wisdom. As I journey through life, help me to live in complete harmony with You.

More Valuable Than Rubies

As women, many of us struggle with our self-concepts. We live in a world that tells us we have to measure up to multiple standards. We have to prove our worth again and again, in all sorts of ways.

First of all, we have to look a certain way. We need to have bodies that are shaped according to the standards our society considers beautiful (no matter how impossible they may be for most women to attain). Our hair needs to be in style, our clothes fashionable, and our faces perfectly made up. When we step on the scales, we need to see numbers that are closer to one hundred than two hundred!

At the same time, we need to juggle all the roles we fill. Many of us are working women who need to compete in the professional world. We have to be on time, be efficient, keep our cool, pay attention, work to get to the top, and earn enough to help support our families. At the same time, though, we need to be able to care for our families. We nurture children and older parents. We are faithful and sensitive friends, and we are loving wives. But that's not all! We also have to keep our houses clean. . .prepare meals. . . volunteer at church and in our communities. . .and somehow stay calm through it all. Most of all, we want to make everyone happy. We want to do everything we can to make everyone like us!

When we can't achieve all this—and who can?— our sense of our own value plummets. We compare ourselves to those around us, who all seem to be doing so much better than we are at being pretty, smart, accomplished, loving, and loved women. We become discouraged and full of despair. We doubt our own worth.

But Proverbs 31 doesn't say that our value is based on any of these things. Instead, it says that when we are women of virtue—women of strength and courage—then we are worth more than any jewel. It doesn't say anything at all about our worth depending on how clean our houses are or how much we weigh. Or even on how much other people like us!

God doesn't care about any of the standards we so often use to define ourselves. Whether we are overweight or slender, well dressed or scarecrows, slobs or tidy, professionals or stay-at-home moms, popular or social misfits, we are all equally treasured. We are more valuable than rubies because God has filled us with virtue!

Loving God, You know how hard I try to be everything that's expected of me. I wear myself out working so hard to be good at all the roles I fill. I truly want to be good at each of the jobs I do, both at home and at work. And I want so much to make those I love happy. When I start to focus too much on these things, though, I ask that You remind me to shift my attention to You. Help me to rely on Your perspective instead of society's. Give me confidence in the strength You have given me—strength to love, strength to serve You, strength to do good in the world.

PART II

Her husband has full confidence
in her and lacks nothing of value.
She brings him good, not harm,
all the days of her life.
—VERSES 11–12 NIV

Deep Enough

The husband of the Proverbs 31 woman trusts her completely because she's proven herself trustworthy. At first it's tempting to skip over that statement quickly, thinking to ourselves, *Of course I'm trustworthy. I'd never cheat on my husband. And I do more than my part to make this marriage work. My husband isn't lacking anything, not on my account!* But sometimes we should take another honest look at ourselves. Can our husbands trust us to understand them, even when understanding might ask us to adjust our own thinking or behaviors? Do they lack our respect when it comes to their interests and emotions? Do we ever hurt their feelings? Are we impatient with them, easily irritated? Is it truly our goal to bring our husbands "good, not harm" each and every day?

Many times, I suspect, we're so busy with our many responsibilities that our husbands' needs fall into the background. Instead, we're likely to be far more aware of all the ways we wish they would help us out—and then we feel frustrated and angry if they don't. Our own needs are at the forefront of our consciousness. When we think of our husbands, we often tend to focus on what we get from them emotionally—and we may complain a lot about what we don't get! We may be far less aware of our own shortcomings in the relationship.

This doesn't mean we need to be doormat wives, submissive in the old-fashioned sense of the word. God doesn't ask us to be untrue to our own needs or to deny our God-given identities. We might want to ask ourselves these questions instead: "Is my husband as real to me as I am to myself? Or do I see him as someone I expect to be there at my convenience, someone whose job is to make my life easier? Do I see his needs as being as important as my own? Do I accept him unconditionally?"

Psychologist Carl Rogers referred to "unconditional positive regard" when he wrote about the important components of a healthy relationship. The ability to care about your partner—and communicate your concern without a lot of judgmental stuff thrown in— is the essence of a healthy intimate relationship.

It's not easy, of course. But no one ever said marriage was easy! Being married isn't a decision you can make once and then be done with it. The wedding ceremony does not magically transform us into "married people." Instead, being married is a lifetime process, one we must commit ourselves to again and again. We must choose to be married daily—and that means choosing to go past our own immature, selfish emotions. It means choosing to go deep enough that our husbands can trust us to bring them only good.

God of love, thank You for my husband. Give me strength today to look past my preoccupation with myself. Help me to truly see this man I'm married to. Show me where I have failed to understand him, where I have been too preoccupied with my own concerns to see his. Let me find ways to bring good into his life.

Leap Of Faith

"You're acting like a selfish princess," we used to say to our daughter when she was younger. But I have to admit I have a selfish princess who lives inside me as well. She's the one who always wants to be in control. She wants her husband to make her life easier, not harder. Actually, she kind of treats him like her slave.

And when he doesn't always cooperate, I'm as frustrated and angry as any four-year-old. When my requests turn into demands, however, I'm failing to respect my husband's personhood. He is not my slave; he was not put on earth for my sole convenience. Slavery sees another human being as a mere object, but true love honors that person.

Married partners are called "helpmeets" because they are in fact intended to help each other. I often expect my husband's help—for everything from killing spiders to opening cans—and I admit he seldom asks me for anything in return that I find unreasonable or too demanding. Sometimes he asks me to scratch his back or get him a drink when he's working. Most of the time he doesn't exactly ask, he just hints—like when I haven't made his favorite meal in a while. By the same token, sometimes when we're both in bed, I'll start complaining about how thirsty I am; he'll groan, but he gets up to get me a glass of water.

But those are simple requests. It's easy to look only at them and give myself a pat on the back for being such a good wife. But then another recent event comes to mind.

Our family car needed repairs, and my husband and I had agreed to meet at a certain time at the service station. We would leave the family car, and then I'd take the car he usually drives and drop him off back at work. I then needed to be at an appointment, and I had several other responsibilities I had to fit in before the end of the workday. The schedule I had planned for myself was a tight one, so I was irritated when I arrived at the service station and found that my husband wasn't there. When I called him, he asked me in a brusque voice to wait for him a bit longer.

An hour ticked away. I had to call and cancel my appointment. I kept looking at the time and feeling more and more frustrated. There was no way now I could get everything done that I had to do. I felt totally out of control of my own life, and I resented my husband for doing that to me. By the time he arrived, I was furious.

"How can you be so selfish?" I demanded. "Does it ever occur to you that I have things to do, too?" I may have said a few other things as well.

He gave me a quick, angry answer. His voice was defensive, and he barely looked at me. In fact, he seemed preoccupied, as though he could not have cared less about my disrupted day. *What a jerk*, I thought to myself as I dropped him off at work. We didn't even say good-bye as he got out and hurried back into his workplace.

By the time he came home that night, I was sorry for losing my temper. I was even sorrier when I learned he had been in the middle of a safety crisis at work, something he couldn't discuss until it was over.

But I didn't trust him enough to give him the help he needed without complaint. I wasn't thinking about doing good for him. (Mostly, I was just thinking about how much I wanted to clobber him.)

It doesn't come naturally to lay aside our own personal agendas—especially if we don't see a good reason why we should. Sometimes it means taking a small leap of sheer, blind faith. When we do, we give our husbands reason to have confidence in us.

Dear Jesus, when You were on earth, You were always true to Yourself—and yet at the same time, You gave Yourself in love to others. Show me how to do the same with my husband. May I not be so quick to get angry. Instead, teach me to rely more on Your love, knowing that You will work out everything—even my tight schedule—to the glory of God.

Let Love Flow

How often do you tell your husband you love him? It's a simple habit to form—and the more often we say the words, the more secure our husbands will feel. It's a habit that pays off in other ways as well.

Sometimes we get in vicious circles where we snap at our husbands. . .they feel hurt and exasperated, so they give an angry retort. . .we're hurt by their angry voices, so we go on the defensive. . .and the circle goes around and around until something or someone breaks it. But we can choose to form "loving circles" instead. Psychologists have found that the more often we express love, the more loving we tend to feel. This productive and kind cycle strengthens the feeling that inspires the words, and on and on.

We don't have to wait for our husbands to be the first to start these loving cycles. The more we express our love to our husbands, the more likely they are to respond with their own expressions of love, forming another beneficial and creative circle to replace the vicious circles we all fall into so easily.

Marriage is an opportunity to let God's love flow through us. Our culture usually looks at things differently; most people spend their lives looking for ways that others can be of use to them. We may have entered marriage with that same attitude, expecting our husbands to make us feel loved, rather than seeking opportunities to demonstrate our love to them. Often, we wait to be told we're loved before we'll respond in kind. Even within the marriage commitment, we want to know we're secure before we'll lay our hearts out where they might be hurt.

But that's not the way God loves. God's love is completely vulnerable. There are no self-protective barriers around it. It gives without thought of return. It doesn't wait for us to love God back. It simply pours into our lives, no matter how often we reject it and turn away from it, no matter how many times we're too focused on our concerns to even notice it.

What would happen if we tried to love our husbands that way?

Dear God, each of my days is filled with Your love. Everywhere I turn, I see Your love—in the world of nature, in my friends, in my family, in Your Spirit filling my heart. You never hold back Your love. You give it freely, unconditionally, endlessly. I know I can never hope to love as perfectly as You do, but may I seek to model my love for my husband after Your love. May I be quick to express love, slow to express anger and impatience. May I be thoughtful of his needs, as sensitive to his feelings as I am to my own. Help me to be a channel through which Your love can flow to my husband.

Warm, Sweet Junes

Our romantic fairy-tale view of marriage leads us to expect that once two people marry, they will be happy forevermore, end of story. So when we run into long stretches of boredom or unhappiness, we doubt our love. After all, according to the dictates of our culture, if we're not happy, then something is wrong—and we often assume the fault lies with our husbands. Clearly, they don't love us enough! If they did, we'd be happy. We'd still feel that same love and joy we felt at the beginning of our relationships. That sense of "something wrong" can make us build walls around our hearts. We feel as though we need to withdraw from our husbands, put up our defenses. It seems perfectly sensible to place our own needs first. We lose confidence in our husbands—and in return, we give them reason to lose confidence in us.

These times come to even the strongest marriages, particularly during the early years, before experience gives us greater perspective. As the years go by, though, we may learn that, like the seasons, married love has cycles. Sometimes our marriages may seem as cold and dead as January—but if we wait, if we're patient, spring always comes once more. Then we may find ourselves surprised—and delighted—to be falling in love with our husbands all over again. It would be easier to run away the first time November's chilly gray skies settle over our marriages. But just think of all the warm, sweet Junes we would miss if we did!

Romantic books and movies don't prepare us for

marriage's reality. From the time we were children, we were raised on the words, "And they lived happily ever after." No one ever mentioned that happiness is hard work. But the truth is, after we've fallen into each other's arms and declared our mutual passion, after we've gone still further and said, "I do," that's when the real story begins. And that story is full of joy and tenderness—but it's also full of frustration and self-discipline.

By definition, marriage requires that two distinct entities become one. No matter how much in love we are, making two entirely separate individuals into a single unit is not an easy task. R. C. Sproul once said, "If you imagined your mother married to your father-in-law, and your father married to your mother-in-law, you'd have a good picture of the dynamics of marriage." I dearly love both my own parents and my in-laws, but that quote always makes me smile, for it creates an image in my mind of two preposterous unions. I don't smile nearly as wide, though, when Sproul's quote becomes plain in my own marriage.

A peaceful union is hard to achieve, and oneness is not something that happens overnight. The marriage ceremony does not magically erase the differences between husband and wife, and neither does it cancel our selfish natures. Married harmony requires instead an acceptance that conflict is bound to occur; it also requires a commitment to ongoing reconciliation—for a lifetime. That commitment creates a safe and secure place, a place where our husbands can trust us, where we can do them good—and receive good in return.

Loving Lord, I ask that You strengthen my commitment to my husband. May I not simply go through the motions of marriage, out of habit. May I actively seek to do him good, even in the bleak, cold days of our marriage's winters.

Practical Hope

The apostle Paul says that faith, hope, and love are the three things that last (1 Corinthians 13:13). We talk a great deal about faith and love, but we often tend to skim over hope, as though it were somehow not quite as practical as the other two, not essential to our daily lives. In reality, though, hope is immensely practical, especially in a marriage. It's the thing that carries us forward, even when our married love may seem dry and dead. Hope is the bridge that gets us over the dark times. It's what keeps us believing in the future, no matter what the present looks like.

But we need to be open to being surprised. If our hope is based on the expectation that things are going to work out exactly the way we want them to, we're bound to be disappointed and disillusioned. Hope doesn't mean counting on getting your own way. Instead, it means trusting that God is in whatever comes.

Sometimes our spouses change in unexpected ways. The men we thought we married may seem very different from the men we're married to today. Hope leaves room for those changes.

I am not the same person I was when I got married. I have gained self-confidence and developed talents I was once afraid to explore. And on the downside, I weigh about twenty pounds more than I did on the day I said, "I do." I am grateful my husband's love is flexible enough that he can give me room to grow and change within the safe space of our marriage commitment. Even when changes startle him or make him uncomfortable—like when my job takes me to faraway places without him—he makes an effort to give me the space I need to grow. He's proud of me. Can I give him the same level of commitment?

If we hold on to the images we have in our heads of our husbands and refuse to let them go, we are not giving our husbands reason to have confidence in our love. Married love is a promise that creates a shelter where each partner has room to stretch, to spread out, to grow into the people God wants us to be.

One reason some marriages fail is because partners are bored. Spouses assume they know everything there is to know about each other—and familiarity breeds both contempt and boredom. In reality, though, we will never know everything there is to know about our husbands. We may see only our images of who they are and assume we know all there is to know—and all the while we fail to perceive the amazing quirks and startling changes that hide behind the familiar faces.

When our marriages seem to be failing us, maybe we don't need new spouses but new eyes! When we are willing to see with the eyes of hope, to see who our husbands really are (instead of the old, familiar images of them we've been looking at), we may be surprised by what we see. Hope can be a bridge that leads to new and amazing places.

Lord, help me to see my husband and
our marriage with the eyes of hope.
Give me confidence in You so that my
husband may have confidence in me.

See More Clearly

Living as closely to another person as we do in marriage, we can't help but rub each other the wrong way. We have prickly egos that clash against each other. Marital conflict is normal and even healthy, but it also can be hurtful and destructive. When we give in to our anger, most of us tend to wield it like a weapon against our husbands. We go for the throat, trying to do as much damage as we can. When we do, our conflicts are not constructive but the opposite.

Anger is a little like a spade. A spade can be used as a deadly weapon—but it can also be used to turn the earth for a new garden. Inevitably, we will be at odds with our husbands from time to time—but we do not need to attack them with our anger. Instead, used properly, anger can be the tool that opens the soil of our marriages so fresh life can grow.

Most of us wives have lists we keep in the back of our heads, itemizing our husbands' irritating characteristics, the ones we'd most like to change. It's all too easy to focus on the ways we'd like our husbands to be different. Many of our frustrations are even legitimate! Our husbands certainly aren't perfect (any more than we are).

An abusive husband is something different. In that case, where a wife's well-being is in danger, she needs to take whatever steps she needs to take to be safe. For many of us, though, our husbands fail us in the normal, everyday ways all human beings fail each other.

Insisting that they change generally only creates

resentment on their part and frustration on ours. We cannot force our husbands (or anyone else) into the shape we'd like—even when we know that shape would be far healthier. . .or more spiritual. . .or more conducive to family peace. Even when we know we're right!

The truth is, our husbands' most irritating qualities may never go away. Once we accept that, once we stop wasting all our energy on lost causes, we can look at ourselves and see how we can think or behave differently instead. Ultimately, the only people we can change are ourselves.

As husbands and wives, we come to each other with different backgrounds that formed us into the people we are today. No matter how much we love each other, we can't erase the shapes heredity and environment have given us. Instead, maybe we should simply accept that we are who we are. God was a part of the forces that influenced our identities—and if we commit our lives to God, grace will continue to work in our lives. When we accept our husbands unconditionally, we give them reason to have confidence in us; we have opportunities to do them good.

We'll still get angry with them. That anger can be creative rather than destructive, though, when it doesn't shake the foundation of our commitment to our husbands. It can give us opportunities to talk with our spouses, to see things more clearly.

Lord, I give You the anger I sometimes feel at my husband. May I not use it as a weapon against him, trying to change him to be who I want. I surrender myself and my marriage to You.

Bridge Between Two Hearts

The apostle Paul advises us to live at peace with everyone, as much as we possibly can (Romans 12:18). This certainly applies to our marriages. Our commitment to peace is one more way we can give our husbands reason to have confidence in us.

Sometimes, though, it is not possible to live at peace with our husbands. We can try to understand their motives and their actions; we can listen intently to their concerns; we can change our approach and our priorities to accommodate their needs and preferences. And after all our efforts, we may still find conflict within our marriages.

A marriage is like a bridge between two hearts. It takes a commitment from both parties to bridge the gap between you. That gap is normal and healthy—marital unity does not take away the fact that you are two individuals—but when the bridge across the gap breaks, there is a limit to what one person can do to repair the damage.

We should, of course, do all we can to repair the breach. If we have hurt our husbands, we need to ask their forgiveness. If we have broken trust, we must commit ourselves to rebuilding it. But having done all this, if our husbands don't want to repair their ends of the bridge, we can only accept—and respect—their decisions. We cannot control them in this situation, any more than we can in other situations. (Again, we're not talking about abusive husbands, whose hurtful behaviors should *never* be accepted.)

It hurts to feel as though our love is rejected. If we think of our marriage as having seasons, a situation like this—where our husbands are no longer committed to making our marriages work—seems like a winter that will never end. Our natural tendency is to hurt when we've been hurt. We may want to punish our husbands and protect our hearts by pulling down our ends of the marriage bridge.

Can we instead put our hope in God and continue to love our husbands? Can we be willing to endure hurt and still seek to do our husbands good? Marriage can be painful, but even at its worst—when peace seems gone from it forever—we can be like the grain of wheat Jesus talked about in the Gospels. Until the grain fell into the earth and died, it could never grow and be fruitful. By the same token, when we allow our hearts to break, God's creative power is free to work, both within us and within our marriages.

Work in my marriage, I pray, Lord, even when I feel hurt and rejected. May I rely on You for my security. Bring hope to what seems hopeless. Give me strength to love even when I feel unloved. Use me even now to do my husband good.

PART III

*She selects wool and flax
and works with eager hands.*
—VERSE 13 NIV

Keep At It!

The Proverbs 31 woman selects wool and flax and works with eager hands. In our modern-day world, what we can learn from this? A lot of us are knitters—and some of us are weavers and embroiderers—but I don't think the lesson here has to do merely with handwork!

First of all, the Proverbs 31 woman picks what she needs to do a job. She doesn't wait for someone to give her what she needs. Instead, she goes ahead and gets it for herself. She has enough confidence in her own intelligence and abilities that she can take the initiative.

Next, she works with eager hands. This tells me she doesn't just begin the job. She keeps at it. I sometimes have trouble with that. I begin jobs with excitement—and then it fades as the work grows old. I lose interest. I start to procrastinate.

"Now finish the work," Paul wrote in his second letter to the Corinthians, "so that your eager willingness to do it may be matched by your completion of it" (8:11 NIV). He was talking to the church at Corinth about their willingness to give to those in need. It was a worthy project—like so many of ours—that was started eagerly, with passion and commitment. And then somewhere along the way, the church people lost interest.

My life is full of abandoned, unfinished projects. Half-sewn quilts, half-written books, half-straightened closets. Of course, not every job is worth finishing. We don't need to feel a sense of false guilt if we realize partway through something that our time could be better spent somewhere else. But we do need to examine our reasons for moving on. Are we giving up this work because we lack confidence in our ability to finish it well—so it's easier to walk away than to fail? Are we abandoning a project because it has turned out to not be as rewarding as we hoped—and by that do we really mean that it is demanding more from us than we want to give? Does it ask us to die to ourselves in ways that feel uncomfortable?

If God was in the birth of this work, then chances are God wants to be in the completion of it as well. Can we lay aside our need to do things perfectly and leave the results in God's hands? Can we be willing to work hard even when it's no longer fun? If we can, then one day we'll be able to say with Paul, "I have finished my course, I have kept the faith" (2 Timothy 4:7 KJV). And like Jesus, we can say, "My nourishment comes from doing the will of God"—not from being perfect or from having fun while we work!—"and from finishing his work" (John 4:34 NLT).

Forgiving God, give me the strength, the courage, and the humility I need to finish the work to which You call me. May I be willing to work hard—and then leave the final results in Your hands.

Joy In Work

The Hebrew word used by the author of Proverbs 31 for "eager"—*chephets*—means literally "delight, pleasure, longing." In other words, the Proverbs 31 woman takes pleasure in her work, and she longs to give pleasure to others with it. Almost all work has its boring aspects, of course, but God does want us to find joy in the work to which we are called.

One of the works to which God calls us is hospitality—welcoming others into our homes and hearts. This, too, is an occasion when we can seek to model the Proverbs 31 woman. We can look for what we need to do this job—and then carry it out eagerly.

Some of us are born hostesses, and hospitality comes easily to us. Often we follow the models of hospitality we learned from our mothers. My mother was quick to invite people into our home—but she also became tense and flustered each time she prepared for guests. I grew up hating the days when we had company because I knew it would be preceded by hours of frantic busyness, while my mother snapped at all of us to help her clean and cook.

As a result, today when I practice hospitality I tend to be more of a Martha than a Mary. I can relate to the story in Luke where it says, "Martha was distracted by the big dinner she was preparing." When she complained to Jesus that her sister wasn't helping her enough, He said to her, "My dear Martha, you are worried and upset over all these details! There is only one thing worth being concerned about. Mary has discovered it" (Luke 10:38–42 NLT).

The Bible says Martha was the one who had opened her home to Christ—a generous, loving act of hospitality. Yet serving Christ, which should have been a joy, was actually distracting her from her relationship with Him. Maybe she had planned too elaborate a meal, beyond what she could do easily in the time she had. Maybe she had hoped to impress Him with it—not realizing that that sort of thing just didn't impress Jesus.

There are lessons we can all learn from Martha's experience, lessons that the Proverbs 31 woman had apparently already learned:

- ℘ The next time we invite someone into our homes, we shouldn't attempt anything more elaborate than we can handle.
- ℘ We should take joy in hospitality rather than fussing over the details, getting tense and bothered by every little thing that goes wrong.
- ℘ If we turn hospitality into a burden, we shouldn't expect our families to help us carry it—and then feel resentful if they don't.
- ℘ We should remember that guests would rather feel they are our focus rather than any meal, no matter how delicious or elaborate.
- ℘ Our hospitality is also service to Jesus; as we offer our guests food and welcome, we are also loving and welcoming Him.
- ℘ Love doesn't compete. It doesn't look at what someone else is doing and measure our success or failure by another's efforts.
- ℘ When we feel stressed and distracted with our

work, we need to sit at Jesus' feet and listen to His Word. Our work, no matter how well intentioned, is never a substitute for a living relationship with God.

God, You are a generous host, inviting us into Your home and heart. Make me more like You. Give me joy in hospitality.

Eager Hands

I'm still thinking about the Proverbs 31 woman's eager hands. They suggest to me an energy and enjoyment that I don't always bring to my daily chores.

I like to feel that I'm being productive, though— and I'm often so busy that each day has a to-do list that's at least a page long. Then I work my way through it, checking things off as I go. Each check mark gives me a tiny burst of satisfaction. At the end of the day, a good day has lots of check marks, while a bad day has very few. Bad days make me feel frustrated and unproductive. They make me feel as if I wasted time, that I *should* have gotten more done.

But what were the distractions that kept me from checking off the things on my list? They're usually things I couldn't control that came up during the day—a phone call from an old friend who's in a crisis, a child needing me to bring something to school that was forgotten, my husband's car breaking down. Demands from other people got in the way of my to-do list.

I'm far too focused, though, on the end result of my work. I don't have eager hands for the work itself; I just want the satisfaction of getting it done. I don't see my work as being ongoing service to God, service that may not always be what I have in mind and that often includes service to the ones I love. I have my priorities—but they're not necessarily God's priorities.

God doesn't really care all that much how many things are checked off my to-do list at the end of the day! Instead, Jesus makes clear what is most important from God's perspective: "'Love the Lord your God with all your heart and with all your soul and with all your mind.' This is the first and greatest commandment. And the second is like it: 'Love your neighbor as yourself'" (Matthew 22:37–39 NIV).

So instead of assessing my day by the number of check marks on my list, I should be asking myself: Did I love God with all my heart, soul, and mind today? Did I consider others' needs as important as my own? Was everything I did done in love? Did I serve God with glad hands?

> *Give me glad hands, Lord God—hands that are quick to help, quick to give, quick to show love.*

In The Small Moments

Our world values speed—but glad hands are not necessarily fast hands! This goes back to our need to get a lot done in a day. We think that the faster we are, the better we are. But some things cannot be done quickly. Love sometimes takes time.

It's hard to keep this perspective in a world that constantly tells us to move faster. We need to reorient ourselves daily, spending time each morning to consciously align ourselves with divine perspectives. Even if you can't find time in your busy mornings for alone time, take a few minutes before you get up or while you're in the shower to turn your heart to God.

When we're stressed with our work—whatever it is—we often fall asleep thinking about the work that needs to be done, and we wake up still thinking about it. We've taken our stress to bed with us, and it's no wonder our bodies are exhausted and our emotions are stretched. It's hard to have glad hands in the midst of tension!

Instead, we might consider making a habit of falling asleep in prayer and waking up in prayer. As the psalmist says, "Meditate in your heart upon your bed, and be still" (4:4 NASB). If we take time, even a few sleepy moments, to simply "be still, and know that [God is] God" (Psalm 46:10 KJV), our days will go better. During these moments, it helps to consciously relax our bodies and let the tension slip away from our muscles. We will find a tiny pocket of peace, a place where we can discover that God "maketh the storm a calm, so that the waves thereof are still" (Psalm 107:29 KJV).

Don't think of time with God as one more thing to check off your to-do list! And don't set yourself unrealistic goals for times of devotion. If you're the mother of young children, you're very likely already sleep deprived—telling yourself you'll get up even a half hour earlier for morning devotions may not be realistic or even healthy. Instead, learn to turn to God in the small moments—before sleep, in the morning when you wake up, in the shower, while waiting at a red light, anywhere there's a pause in the day's busyness. "Pray in the Spirit on all occasions with all kinds of prayers and requests" (Ephesians 6:18 NIV). Those few seconds will reorient your thoughts—and help you remember that love is always God's priority. You'll return to your work with glad hands.

You know how busy my days are, Lord. Thank You that even if I forget You, You never forget me. Remind me throughout the day to turn my heart to You. Be my companion, moment by moment, I pray, so that I may do my work with gladness.

All In God's Presence

God knows the reality of our lives. If we've been up all night with a new baby or a sick toddler or a child who's been having nightmares (or all three!), then He knows we may truly need that hour of sleep more than we need to be reading the Bible or praying. Our hands aren't going to be very glad as we do our work if we're exhausted.

As women, we've often set standards for ourselves that are impossibly high. We forget we have a God who loves us like a parent, a God who knows our physical, emotional, and spiritual needs better than we do ourselves. God doesn't ask most of us to be martyrs; but He does want us to have a living relationship with Him.

Brother Lawrence, the seventeenth-century author of *The Practice of the Presence of God*, has some practical advice for those of us who are trying to be like the Proverbs 31 woman. He spent most of his life in the busy monastery kitchen; his days were hectic, filled with the ordinary hustle and bustle of providing food for a community—just like many of our days. And yet Brother Lawrence could write, "These busy times are no different for me than prayer times. In my kitchen's noise and clatter, while several people are all calling for different things, I possess God just as peacefully as if I were on my knees."

To keep our hands glad and our hearts loving, we need a constant sense of God's presence with us. But, this living, everyday awareness of God doesn't happen easily; it requires discipline. Brother Lawrence wrote that he spent ten years of practice before he began to feel God's presence with him moment by moment—and even then he often found that distractions came between him and his Lord. But he didn't allow these distractions to make him feel guilty; each time he realized his mind had wandered away from God, he simply and immediately went back into Christ's presence. He wrote:

> I worshipped Him as often as I could, keeping my mind focused on His holy presence and calling my attention back whenever I found myself being distracted. This exercise was not easy, and yet I continued in it, in spite of how hard it was, without worrying or feeling guilty every time my thoughts wandered. I worked at this all day long, not only during prayer times, for at all times, every hour, every minute, even in the midst of my busiest times, I drove out of my mind anything that might distract me from thoughts of God. . . . Practicing this over and over, it becomes a habit, and the presence of God becomes the natural condition for us.[1]

Someone who knew Brother Lawrence wrote of him, "His prayer was simply a sense of God's presence. . . . When his prayer time was over, nothing changed, because he still continued to be with God." This continual, living awareness of God with us, intimately involved with our ordinary lives, is what we need as

1. Ellyn Sanna, *Brother Lawrence: Christian Zen Master*. (Vestal, NY: Anamchara Books, 2011).

busy women. Seeking Brother Lawrence's way of life asks that we live our entire lives, from dirty diapers to grocery trips, from peanut butter and jelly sandwiches to car pools, all in God's presence.

God, I know I can never leave Your presence. May I live in that awareness. Each moment of even my busiest days, may I serve You gladly.

Precious Resources

Maybe one of the reasons the Proverbs woman could have glad hands was because she had already identified the resources she would need to carry out her work. In her case, it was wool and flax—in our case, it might be time, people, space, education, certain technology, physical strength, or supplies. You can't complete your work if you don't have what you need to do it!

We all have varying amounts of various resources. Here are some categories to consider. List the resources you have in these areas.

- ☞ Spiritual: Are you depending on God for strength and support? Do you feel that God has led you to this work?
- ☞ Financial: Do you have the money you need for the job?
- ☞ Emotional: Can you cope with the emotional demands of this work?
- ☞ Mental: Do you have the intellectual skills you need to meet your goal? These might include the abilities to solve problems, communicate verbally and in writing, and understand others' words.
- ☞ Physical: Are you healthy enough to take on this work right now? Are you physically strong enough for the work?
- ☞ Support systems: Do you have friends, family, a community that will back you up in this

work? Are there people you can turn to for help when you need it?

Take a clear-eyed look at the work you've taken on—and then see how it matches up with the points above. Do you have the resources you need to do it? If not, where can you find what you need? Do you need to learn something you don't know (by reading a book, attending a class, taking an online tutorial)? Do you need to consider spending some money on a better computer or vehicle? Are there resources you have that you may not have even noticed? For example, are there people who would be willing to help you (by teaching you, carpooling with you, lending you something)? Who do you know who has specialized knowledge in the area where you're working? Who might share your passion for this work? Who might have talents to complement your own?

Don't forget that time is also one of our most important resources. Each day is like a container into which you can put many things—but not an infinite number of things! Think about what your priorities are each day. What is the best use of this precious resource?

Don't set yourself unrealistic expectations. Make sure the goals you've set yourself are achievable because you have the resources you'll need. At the same time, learn to have confidence in your own ability to pick and choose wisely. You will make mistakes along the way, but mistakes are only learning opportunities. Don't let fear of failure take the gladness from your hands!

God, I give my work to You. May I be wise and discerning as I consider what resources I need to achieve my goals. Guide me, I pray.

PART IV

She is like the merchant ships,
bringing her food from afar.
—VERSE 14 NIV

Spiritual Nourishment

The author of Proverbs compares his ideal woman to a ship that sails to far ports in order to import food to her homeland. What does this metaphor mean to us today?

Perhaps what we can learn here from the Proverbs 31 woman is this: we need to be willing to go outside our normal habits and routines to find the nourishment we need. We need to let God out of the box where we may have put Him and allow Him to surprise us. Saint Benedict, a sixth-century Christian, advised his followers to "listen with the ear of the heart," paying close attention to where God might be directing their attention. We, too, need to listen for God calling us to unfamiliar places where He wants to feed us from His rich supply of nourishment.

Often, however, when the demands of daily life deplete our strength and energy, when life seems so busy that there's barely time to sleep or eat, the first thing we eliminate from our lives is the very thing we need the most: spiritual nourishment. Author Rick Warren writes, "If you were a construction contractor, you wouldn't consider sending out a guy who hadn't eaten anything in two weeks. If you were a commander in the Army, you wouldn't send a person into battle who hadn't eaten in a month. Right? We need to feed ourselves to have the strength to accomplish the tasks ahead of us."[2] As women, though,

---

2. Rick Warren. "Spiritual Food for Spiritual Strength," *Daily Hope*, May 21, 2014, http://rickwarren.org/devotional/english/spiritual-food-for-spiritual-strength.

we're often so busy offering physical and emotional nourishment to others that we forget to feed our own hearts!

The things that nourish your heart may not be what nourishes someone else's. Pay attention to your own needs—and give your heart the food it needs! There are obvious ways to nourish our spirits, and we shouldn't abandon these, of course. Prayer, reading scripture, and getting together with other believers are all essential pieces of spiritual nourishment. But God can also feed your heart in other ways. Listen to music that opens up your soul. Make opportunities to appreciate nature. Go to an art museum and feast your eyes. Read poetry or fiction that stirs your imagination. Be open to trying new things—but don't force yourself to consume "food" that doesn't truly nourish you. Avoid spiritual junk food, like TV shows that offer you little real nourishment.

Just as our bodies need food to be healthy, so do our souls. Are we willing to make an effort to see that our souls are fed—or are we so busy that we're starving ourselves?

Lord, I need Your nourishment. Show me where to go to get it. Remind me that I cannot do the work to which You've called me when I'm spiritually weak and hungry. Show me all the ways You seek to feed my heart.

In The Desert Times

Sometimes we go through periods of spiritual and emotional famine in our lives. No matter how far we travel in our "merchant ship," we can't seem to find the nourishment our hearts crave. Everywhere we turn, everything looks dry and brown. Drought lies over our lives.

Scripture indicates that these times of spiritual famine and drought are normal. They come to every life. The drought may be caused by disappointment or failure. It might be caused by grief and sorrow— or by the pain of rejection. Sometimes the drought and famine seem as though they will last forever. We wonder if we'll ever find spiritual and emotional food again.

At times like these, we may blame ourselves. We feel as though there's something wrong, we wonder what we did to cause this famine, and we seek desperately to find ways to fix it. Instead, we might try accepting the desert times rather than trying to make them go away. When we do, we may discover what our hearts are truly craving.

Physical hunger is our bodies' way of telling us that they need something; we need to take action to feed them. Spiritual hunger is also a message that we need to seek out the sustenance we truly need. If the old ways of nourishment are gone—or they no longer satisfy the way they once did—that's a good sign that something in our lives needs to change. Our longing for nourishment and fulfillment might just be the "ship" that carries us to a new and deeper understanding of God and ourselves. It could be God's invitation to seek our hearts' food somewhere new.

During these desperate, painful times, we come to God in a new way. The ship of our heart travels to unexplored and unfamiliar places. All the old distractions we thought were our souls' food are gone. There may be nothing whatsoever wrong with them, but now that they've disappeared, we can develop an appreciation for the pure food of God's Spirit. During these famine times, God feeds us directly from His own heart, if only we will let Him.

In the midst of these times of spiritual hunger and emotional pain, we discover the deepest communion with God. We will find that we have sailed farther than we have ever before gone in the ocean of His love—and we have found there greater nourishment than we ever knew existed. "God will meet all your needs according to the riches of his glory in Christ Jesus" (Philippians 4:19 NIV).

Loving God, I am thankful that I can depend on You to always supply the nourishment I need most. Help me to trust You, even when my life seems dry and barren, lacking food of any sort. Take my eyes off all the things I lack and long for—and instead, teach me to fix my focus on You. I know that in You I will have everything I need.

Bread From Heaven

Jesus told us that when it comes right down to it, He Himself is the food we need most. He is the "bread from heaven" (John 6:32–33). We need to "eat" Jesus. We need to ingest Him so that He can nourish each particle of our bodies, providing us with the energy to live our lives, to grow, and to be the people He calls us to be. "I am the bread of life," Jesus said; "whoever comes to me shall not hunger" (John 6:35 ESV). He is the only permanent satisfaction for all that we long for. As we enter into an intimate relationship with Him, we allow Him to nourish our hearts.

Jesus is the Word spoken by God—the expression of God's identity in human flesh—and when we hear this Word who is Jesus, we accept Him into our minds, our hearts, our spirits. Just as the food we eat changes us physically, so the Word will change us. We will look at life differently. We will begin to live and love like Jesus.

The apostle Paul wrote to the church at Philippi, "Let this mind be in you, which was also in Christ Jesus" (Philippians 2:5 KJV). This means that when we consume Jesus, the Bread of Heaven, we absorb this mind, this attitude, this heart. We take into ourselves the thinking of Jesus, the attitudes of Jesus, His way of acting.

One of the places in the Gospels where we can turn to learn the mind of Jesus is the Beatitudes in Matthew 5:3–10. These verses are what Jesus had to say about the sort of person who pleases His Father.

> "God blesses those who are poor and realize
>   their need for him,
>   for the Kingdom of Heaven is theirs.
> God blesses those who mourn,
>   for they will be comforted.
> God blesses those who are humble,
>   for they will inherit the whole earth.
> God blesses those who hunger and thirst
>   for justice,
>   for they will be satisfied.
> God blesses those who are merciful,
>   for they will be shown mercy.
> God blesses those whose hearts are pure,
>   for they will see God.
> God blesses those who work for peace,
>   for they will be called the children of God.
> God blesses those who are persecuted
>   for doing right,
>   for the Kingdom of Heaven is theirs." (NLT)

These verses also tell us what we should be hungering for most: justice! We need to take our eyes off our own needs and focus them on others' needs. We live in a culture that encourages us to seek that which strokes our own egos first and foremost, so this may indeed be a far-off land for many of us to consider. But if we want to truly absorb Jesus into our very being, then we will begin to say with Him, "My nourishment comes from doing the will of God, who sent me, and from finishing his work" (John 4:34 NLT).

Jesus, feed me Yourself. When I seek to satisfy my heart's hunger in other ways, remind me that only You can truly fill the emptiness in my heart.

Giving And Receiving

I suspect the Proverbs 31 woman didn't keep her nourishment all to herself. She brought it back to her family and her community. She shared it with those around her, and they, too, were nourished. Then they in turn could nourish others. Nourishment is intimately connected to an endless process of giving and receiving.

The natural world offers us countless examples of this web of interconnected life. In a thousand different ways, the world is enmeshed in a vast web of giving and receiving. Plants, for example, produce the oxygen animals need to live; animals breathe it in, and then they breathe out the carbon dioxide plants need to survive. Both plant life and animal life are mutually nourished by one another. Each ecosystem on earth is alive with connections between organisms, each one dependent on the others. Remove one, and the nourishment of all the others will suffer.

The Bible teaches us that the same principle applies to our spiritual lives. We cannot live if we are unconnected to others. Others depend on us for nourishment, just as we depend on them. We each have something to offer to the whole. The apostle Paul put it like this:

> "Even as the body is one and yet has many members, and all the members of the body, though they are many, are one body, so also is Christ. . . . And the eye cannot say to the hand, 'I have no

*need of you'; or again the head to the feet, 'I have
no need of you.' . . . And if one member suffers,
all the members suffer with it; if one member
is honored, all the members rejoice with it"* (1
Corinthians 12:12, 21, 26 NASB).

Sometimes we may need to travel alone to far
lands, away from those we love, in order to find the
sustenance our hearts need. But then we must come
back and share the food. "Feed my sheep," Jesus
told Peter (John 21:16 KJV), and we, too, are called to
feed those who are in our lives: our children, our
husbands, our friends, our neighbors. If we try to keep
it to ourselves, we will find it no longer satisfies our
hearts. We are meant to send out to others that which
we have taken in—and open our hearts to what they
can offer in turn, so that we, too, may be nourished.

As long as we are alive, our bodies never stop
needing food. In a similar way, God's network of need
and sustenance, hunger and food has no beginning or
end. Our nourishment is interconnected. What feeds
me will ultimately feed you as well—and what feeds
you will also feed me. This is the way the entire body
of Christ grows strong and healthy.

*Generous God, I ask that You feed my heart the food that
it needs most—and may I then offer sustenance to
all those I encounter. Use me to feed Your sheep.*

PART V

She gets up while it is still night;
she provides food for her family
and portions for her female servants.
—VERSE 15 NIV

The Value Of Our Work

That Proverbs 31 woman, she sure is busy! Sometimes I kind of hate her. Getting up while it's still dark out so she can make breakfast and lunch and dinner for her household. . .doesn't she have better things she could be doing? Couldn't her husband do some of the food providing?

Personally, I am often ambivalent about my role as a food provider. It seems such a thankless task, a job that has to be done over and over, day after day, week after week. And what am I left with each and every time? A dirty kitchen I have to clean! Making food and cleaning house are endless tasks that never stay done.

My husband and I struggle to divvy up the household chores fairly—if I cook, he cleans the kitchen, and vice versa—but it *is* a struggle. We shared diaper changing when our babies were little— although I'm fairly sure I changed two diapers for every one he did—and he does his share of the laundry. But I suspect he's never, ever cleaned a toilet in his entire life, and he doesn't really understand that refrigerators and stoves don't stay clean all by themselves.

Certain assumptions about who is responsible for meal-making and housecleaning are still deeply ingrained in many of us—and at the same time, as modern women we may resent those assumptions. I can't help but be annoyed by the commercial images of smiling women who apparently find their greatest joy in washing their kitchen floors and serving up easy packaged meals to their families. (According to a 2008 study from the University of New Hampshire, only about 2 percent of commercials showed men doing domestic tasks.) Personally, I often do these household chores grudgingly. And please don't ask me to get up while it's still night to do them!

The Proverbs 31 woman, however, is not downtrodden! She is a strong, capable person, despite the fact that she lived within a patriarchal culture. In Bible times, the division of labor was both clearer and less loaded with value judgments than it is today. The author of Proverbs does not consider his ideal woman to be a second-rate person, one step up from a servant. Taking care of a household was significant and fulfilling work, and it gave dignity and identity to women. Wealthy households were enormous, and the woman who organized the physical needs of all these people had to use as much skill and intelligence as any modern-day corporate executive.

Feeding and caring for a household is important work. It is a reflection of a God who ceaselessly attends to our needs. As humans, we may grow tired of doing the same chores over and over (making the same recipes, setting the same table, washing the same dishes), but God never tires of blessing us again and again. "Repetition," wrote Søren Kierkegaard, "is the daily bread which satisfies with benediction." The Proverbs 31 woman knew the value of her work. Do we?

Loving God, I ask that You help me to see the value of my household work. May I do it in service to You and in love for my family.

Rest

There aren't enough hours in a day.

If you think about that sentence, it's kind of silly. Days have just the right amount of hours for the world of nature; our bodies' cycles depend on regular periods of activity and sleeping, and yet we seem to think the days should somehow expand to meet our convenience. That can't happen of course, not really, but we try to accomplish it by following the Proverbs 31 woman's example: we steal hours from the night and add them to our days.

Whether we're working or stay-at-home mothers, we all feel that there's just not enough time to do all the things we *need* to do. From paying bills to making lunches, from walking the dog to transporting children to after-school activities, from helping children to volunteering at church and school, our lives are jam-packed even before we try to add in the responsibilities of a career. We use adjectives like *crunched* and *stretched* and *pressured* to describe our lives, and those words are indications of how painful our stress levels have become. Responsibilities, both big and little, fill each and every moment of our lives.

A recent survey found that 49 percent of women say they don't have enough free time (defined as "time that you spend on yourself, where you can choose to do things that you enjoy"), let alone time to sleep! In fact, 25 percent said they have less than forty-five minutes a day to care for themselves, and 4 percent said they have zero hours of free time. Unexpected tasks—like sick children, unannounced guests, and broken washing machines—can rob whatever time we might have thought we had to recharge our emotional and spiritual batteries. We have no choice, we think, but to steal from our sleep time.

For many of us, life has become a fast-paced marathon that never ends. But marathon runners know they can't keep up that pace forever. Their bodies need time to rest and recover between races. So do we.

Don't let the Proverbs 31 woman's example encourage you to give up your sleep—or heap guilt on your head if you don't! That long-ago woman lived in a world without electricity, which means she probably went to bed with the sun, even if she got up in the dim light before dawn. Later in chapter 31, we learn that she made sure her lamp didn't go out at night, but in Bible times, lamps were used at night in the way we use nightlights today—so that people could see their way if they needed to get up in what would have otherwise been a pitch-dark house; the small flames weren't bright enough to be used so people could continue to work even in the dark.

Clearly this was an energetic, strong woman who didn't flinch from hard work—but that doesn't mean she didn't take care of her own physical, emotional, and spiritual needs. No woman could be as strong as she was if she didn't!

Sometimes, Beloved Friend, You know I feel desperate for more time in my days. Remind me that You give me everything I need, including time. I can relax, knowing that You arrange my days. Help me to leave things undone with a peaceful mind. Instead of plodding mindlessly on and on, give me the energy and determination to make time for sleep and relaxation when I can renew my heart, mind, and body.

Goals

Are you busy or are you productive? They're not necessarily the same thing. The Proverbs 31 woman may have found that early-morning hours are good ones for getting things done—but she uses those hours efficiently. She gets things accomplished!

We've talked about not being *too* goal oriented when we work, but setting yourself realistic goals—so long as you're enjoying the process of reaching them—can help you organize your work more effectively. It can help you evaluate how you are using your time, since being effective is doing the things that will bring you closer to your goals. Sometimes we're busy with a lot of things that don't really get us anywhere. They take up time, they use up energy, but they don't get the job done!

Being "busy" might include checking your e-mail several times each hour. It could mean answering your phone even when you really don't have time for a conversation. It could mean talking endlessly with a girlfriend when neither of you really has all that much to say. Being obsessive about cleaning our houses or folding our laundry or taking care of our yards can also keep us busy. Countless trips to run errands or transport children can consume our time without helping us meet our goals. Allowing ourselves to be distracted by the television—or Facebook—or any other electronic media can also make our busyness less effective. Letting other people set our goals for us can also keep us busy but not productive.

This *doesn't* mean you should never talk to your friends, never drive your children where they need to go, or not be flexible enough to be available to people when they truly need you. But if you look at your day, how much of it is filled with productive work? What could you cut out without hurting either yourself or anyone else? What could you combine? (For example, could you run to the post office and pick up groceries and drop your kids off at school all in a single trip?) What boundaries could you set around your time to protect you from distractions? (You might, for instance, consider turning off your cell phone when you need to concentrate on a job. You could only check your e-mail at specific times during the day. You could make dates to talk with your friends and ask them to help you meet your work goals by not interrupting the rest of the time unless they truly need you.)

Take a look at your life. How productive are you—and what could you change?

Lord of my life, help me to use my time as efficiently as the Proverbs 31 woman did. Give me the wisdom, energy, and dedication to manage my life more effectively—and may I do it for Your glory.

Productivity

Don't be fooled into thinking you've been productive just because you are busy ten hours a day! If you organize and manage your work more efficiently, you may be surprised to find you can do as much in half the time. Here are some tips for being less busy and more productive:

- Create a daily to-do list each night for the following day.
- Divide the list into chunks of time; be realistic about how much time you will have available and how much time each task will take. Assign a time limit to each task.
- Be like the Proverbs 31 woman and match work that requires focus with times when you know you will have the least distraction.
- Don't try to constantly multitask. Some jobs may lend themselves to being combined with others (for example, you can probably fold laundry at the same time as you quiz your child on her spelling words), but others require your focused attention.
- Set priorities. Which tasks are urgent? Which are important but not urgent? Which are things that you need to get done eventually, as time allows?
- Which two items on your to-do list do you absolutely have to get done no matter what comes up? Be flexible enough to let the other

items go if you have to, so long as those two most important tasks are accomplished.

↬ Use your to-do list as your action plan. Read it over in the morning and refer to it throughout the day so that it keeps you moving along, instead of spending too much time on one task.

↬ Get a friend to be your accountability partner. It helps to have someone to report your progress to so that your plans for being more productive don't get lost and forgotten in the busyness!

Of course, no matter how organized we are or hard we try, we can never control all the factors that may interrupt our days. In the end, it's simply something each of us must balance: doing the best we can to be productive while leaving the ultimate outcome of our efforts in God's hands. Some days we'll do better than others. None of us are perfect, and we all get distracted and overwhelmed. When we do, beating ourselves up for it won't make us more productive! Feeling this sort of false guilt is truly a waste of time. Instead, we need to learn to simply fix our eyes once more on Jesus, the author and finisher of our faith.

Help me today, Lord Jesus, to get done the
things that truly need doing. Give me the faith
to leave the rest in Your hands.

"Make Haste Slowly"

We live in a hurry-up world. The Proverbs 31 woman's culture was far different. She held high standards for herself, but she wasn't trying to measure up to a culture that demanded that she be constantly pulled in different directions, while at the same time telling her to go faster, faster, faster! She could do her work efficiently, with strength and wisdom, because she wasn't exhausted by trying to keep up the marathon pace of a modern woman's life.

Today we all complain about being too busy and not having enough time, but we also take it for granted that that's just the way life has to be. We feel helpless to change it. Our world doesn't offer us many tools for living differently, and so we have to shape them for ourselves.

Cultures earlier in human history, however, were wiser than we are today. The ancient Romans had a phrase that's often translated as "Make haste slowly." In other words, take your time to do the job right. Don't let yourself be so rushed that you lose the focus that peace of mind brings.

Roman coins were even minted that bore the images of a crab and a butterfly as symbols of slowness and speed, reminding people that money is not made with reckless haste but with thoughtful attention. Later, during the Renaissance, workers used other visual symbols to remind them of the wisdom of making haste slowly: a rabbit in a snail shell; a lizard with a fish; a turtle with ship's sails on its back; and a dolphin entwined around an anchor. The sixteenth-century theologian Erasmus complimented someone he knew with these words: "Making haste slowly, he has acquired as much gold as he has reputation, and richly deserves both." "Make haste slowly" is also a Japanese saying that means to advance and grow, but to do so with thought and care.

How can we, too, learn to make haste slowly? Perhaps one way is to simply keep a quiet place in our minds, no matter how busy our days may be, a place where we can withdraw to be at peace with God, a place where we can rest even in the midst of the busyness. Keeping our mental focus, our sense of perspective, will take away the sense that we are constantly rushed. While our minds and bodies are hard at work, our hearts can relax in the Spirit's sure and steady flow.

Is there a visible image that will remind you today to make haste slowly? You might consider creating that image (sketching it or making it on the computer—or even allowing your child to draw it for you) and then placing it where it will be a daily reminder to you.

Lord, may I never go too fast for Your Spirit. Help me not to worry so much about keeping pace with the world's demands, so long as I am keeping pace with You.

PART VI

She considers a field and buys it;
out of her earnings she plants a vineyard.
—VERSE 16 NIV

Thoughtful Decisions

The Proverbs 31 woman is a clear-eyed businessperson who knows how to use her money wisely. When it says she "considers" a field, this means she is giving it some time and thought. She doesn't do things on impulse.

At one time or another, we've all made impulsive, poor spending choices. The lesson that the Proverbs 31 woman has for us is to slow down and think before purchasing. It's okay to spend money for the things we need—but we should make it a personal rule not to buy *anything* on impulse. Various strategies can help us out. For example:

- Make a list before you go to the grocery store of the things you really need.
- When you go to the mall, don't wander aimlessly; go only to the stores that have whatever it is you need to buy.
- Make a budget. Budgets are simply a wise way to set limits on your spending ahead of time.

If finances aren't tight right now in your household, being careful about your money—as well as all other resources, including your time—means that you have more to invest in other things that can benefit both your families and yourself. The Proverbs 31 woman put her earnings into planting a vineyard, something that would continue to provide her household with benefit and income.

Objects aren't the only things to which we may

commit money or other resources. Sometimes we commit to activities that prove to be expensive. Maybe it's an after-school activity for your kids that requires lots of special clothing or equipment that you have to purchase. Maybe it's simply signing up for something that means you need to spend a lot of gas (and time) on traveling back and forth. This doesn't mean that these activities aren't worthwhile or that you should necessarily say no to them. The Proverbs 31 woman simply reminds us to think first. Will this activity truly benefit my household—or will it put an unnecessary burden on us? As Jesus said, "Don't begin until you count the cost. For who would begin construction of a building without first calculating the cost to see if there is enough money to finish it?" (Luke 14:28 NLT).

Jesus, help me to be as wise as the Proverbs 31 woman when it comes to spending my resources. Bless my efforts and make them fruitful for Your glory.

God-Security

When we think about the "field" and the "vineyard" in Proverbs 31:16, we might also meditate on their meaning as spiritual metaphors. Our soul's resources also need to be considered when we commit to something. As Jesus said, "What do you benefit if you gain the whole world but lose your own soul?" (Mark 8:36 NLT). But we also might think a little about what money means to us spiritually and emotionally.

Think about money for a minute. What is it really? Pieces of paper and round bits of metal? Numbers on a computer screen? A piece of plastic in our wallet? Can you really put your finger on what it *means* when you have X amount of dollars in your account?

Originally, money was simply a convenient way to symbolize bulky things of value. Carrying around a cow or a bag of gold wasn't practical, and so people wrote a literal note that stood for what was owed. Coins were another sort of symbol. Gradually, the world became dependent on this system. People no longer thought of money as representing things of value; now it had a value all its own. Societies around the world gave it a magical importance.

But if we could get back to a more realistic perception of money, we might find we could interact with it more wisely. Money represents human effort. It might be the corn grown by a farmer or a dress made in China, but ultimately human hands made the things we use our money to purchase. Money also represents human work itself—the output of time and energy to produce a product or provide a service. Our world today is so interconnected that money flows around the globe, connecting us all in ways that may not be visible—or equitable—but are necessarily very real.

　When we begin to think of money in these terms, as a symbol for the network of giving and receiving that connects human beings, we may find it loses its power over us. It is no longer "my money" in the same way. We can more easily trust God to provide for our needs and avoid the twin pitfalls of greed and financial fears. We can ask God's blessing on money as it flows to us and from us.

　And we can also see more clearly that "profit" can never be measured totally by dollars and cents, and neither can money purchase the security we long for. True prosperity and security are found only by our souls. They come only from God.

God of abundance, I ask that You change my thinking about money. Help me not to worry so much about it. Help me not to ponder ways I can get more of it. Instead, may I give all my resources—my time, my talents, my physical and emotional energy, my creativity— to You and then trust that You will always supply me with exactly what I need. Remind me that Your blessings can never be measured by dollars and cents.

Spiritual Lives And Finances

We often think of money and spiritual matters as living in two totally separate containers. As much as we love money (and most of us do at some level), we also feel that it's soiled, selfish, something that God hates. Certainly, anything we put ahead of God's place in our hearts is an idol, and valuing the dollars in our bank account more than God's love turns money into something that comes between God and ourselves. But it doesn't necessarily have to be like that.

Strangely, the word *mercy* comes from the same word roots as *market* and *merchant*. It has to do with the exchange of that which is valuable. What if we began to see money as simply a symbol for the presence of mercy in our lives, all the while knowing that God's mercy comes to us in many other forms as well?

When we work joyfully, as the Proverbs 31 woman does, doing what we love and loving what we do, we allow mercy to flow through us to others. When we work not to get ahead or fill our bank accounts with those imaginary numbers but as a creative expression of who we are and what we can offer to the world around us, then we can begin to view money in new ways. It loses its magical power. We can begin to think of it as only a token of prosperity, a way to symbolize the flow of human energy and effort that we hold in our hands with gratitude as we give it to God.

In the end, we can't separate our spiritual lives from our finances. God wants us to see life as an undivided whole that belongs totally to Him. We thank Him for that which we have been given—and we ask that we might give back to the world in tangible form. God wants to use our money only to bless us—and to bless others.

With this sort of readjusted mind-set, we can look again at the Proverbs 31 woman's buying, earning, and investing. The crops grown in her field and the grapes grown in her vineyard were enjoyed by the entire community. She wasn't afraid to use her resources in wise ways that increased not only her prosperity but also the prosperity of the world around her.

Be the Lord of my bank account. Teach me to think of money in new ways. Remind me to be more conscious of the ways in which money connects me to others. May my use of money bless not only my family and me but the entire world as well.

Healthy Financial Perspective

Money is one of the things we worry about most. We forget sometimes that worrying about money makes it into an idol just as much as being greedy! Here are a few more things to keep in mind that will help you begin to have a healthier spiritual relationship with your finances:

- Forgive yourself for past financial mistakes and move on. Most of us have made financial decisions we later regretted—but we don't need to let those mistakes define us for the rest of our lives! If we have been unwise in our finances, it's never too late to let the Proverbs 31 woman become our financial model. We should take time to think about the mistakes we have made, though, and learn from them. What can we do differently next time?

- Don't be a hoarder. Money is also called currency (from the word *current*) because it is meant to flow between people. We take part in its circulation when we buy the things we need (which benefits other human beings who make and sell those things), when we tithe to our churches, and when we give to those in need.

- Pray over your bills while you pay them. Paying bills is often a stressful activity that can put us in a state of anxiety. Instead, we can learn to see this as an opportunity to express our gratitude to God and then give Him our needs one by one. (For example: "Dear God, I am thankful that we have a car to drive. Bless it and keep us safe. As I make my car payment, I put our car in Your hands." "Dear Lord, thank You for giving us electricity to light our home. As I pay my electric bill, I put our lights, our appliances, and all the things in our house that use electricity into Your hands. May each of them be used for Your glory.")

- Discover your true wealth. When we look at our lives carefully, we will find areas where we are truly blessed. I may be in a time of financial uncertainty right now, but my marriage is healthy and strong. You may not have the money you need to buy the new home you long for, but you have an abundance of creative talent. Name these areas of wealth—and then share them generously with the world.

- Most of all, remember that God is sometimes called Providence—and He will provide for your needs.

Lord, may I use all my resources with care and wisdom. Thank You for all You have given me. Show me how to use each blessing to bless others.

Blessings

There's a lot of talk these days about the "prosperity gospel." Outside Christian circles, people talk about *The Secret*. What these both have in common is the idea that God—or the universe—wants us to have all the money and physical blessings we could ever ask for.

It's true that God is waiting to bless us with untold riches—but they're not necessarily financial blessings. When we define prosperity in purely monetary terms, we may find ourselves disappointed.

When that happens, we may become cynical about God's promises. We may doubt that He actually cares for us, and we may turn away from Him. "What good does it do to pray?" we may ask ourselves. "God never answers!"

When we're scared we won't be able to pay our bills, it's hard to focus on spiritual blessings. We feel completely out of control of our own lives, and it's a terrifying feeling. And yet in the midst of the fear, God may have gifts He is longing to give us. He can use even our anxiety to bring us closer to Him. When we are desperate, we can no longer rely on other sources of security. God is all we have left.

When we reach that point—when we truly see, maybe for the first time—that God is *all* we have, we realize that in God we have *everything*. Reaching this point of clarity and vision first requires a decision on our part to simply trust God, regardless of what's going on in the outside world. This kind of faith demands everything from us, a total letting go of our control over our own lives. With Job, we say, "Though He slay me, yet will I trust Him" (Job 13:15 NKJV). We can make the same affirmation that the three Hebrews did who were thrown into the fiery furnace: "If we are thrown into the blazing furnace, the God we serve is able to deliver us from it. . . . But even if he does not," we will not turn our backs on Him (Daniel 3:17–18 NIV).

We might never have reached this fiery place of total surrender without our financial worries— and now, in the midst of the flames, we find that we are still safe! We discover a far greater and wider prosperity than that promised by the Law of Attraction.

"And this same God who takes care of me," wrote Paul to the Philippians, "will supply all your needs from his glorious riches, which have been given to us in Christ Jesus" (4:19 NLT). God knows your deepest need—and He longs to meet you there with the bounty of His love.

Loving Lord, I give my financial situation to You. You know my worries. You know how desperate I feel. Help me to accept the anxiety and see what it has to teach me. Give me the strength to surrender control of my life to You. Increase my faith in You.

PART VII

She sets about her work vigorously;
her arms are strong for her tasks.
—VERSE 17 NIV

A Peaceful Heart

The Proverbs 31 woman is strong. She not only does her work gladly, but she also does it vigorously. I have to confess I don't always feel very vigorous when I go about my work. Many things rob me of my strength. One of the biggest is anxiety. I worry about money. I worry about my kids' health. I worry about my performance at work. I worry about my appearance. Some days I worry about pretty much everything! Worry, however, is being afraid of something that exists only in my imagination. There's no real danger threatening me; I'm just afraid it *will* threaten me. And all the while, God is longing to give me—and you—a peaceful heart so I don't waste my strength on empty fears.

Sometimes the thing that robs our hearts of peace is our dissatisfaction with who we are. We want to be smarter. . .prettier. . .thinner. . .funnier. We compare ourselves to others around us, and we find that we never seem to measure up. We wish we could accomplish as much as our sister seems to in a day or that we could keep our homes as tidy as our neighbor does or that our children would behave as well as our friends' children do. We wish we were better cooks. . . calmer. . .more skillful at our careers. . .more creative. We wish our hair looked better! And we worry and fuss over each of these things.

When Jesus hears our minds chattering along like this, He probably longs to whisper, "Shush!" As the Keeper and Guardian of our peace, He asks us to simply take from Him the gift of ourselves. He wants us to humbly accept the people we are—and then offer those people, with all their imperfections, back to Him. He wants us to make peace with ourselves as we are so that we can take on the tasks He has given us.

What stands in our way when we try to reach out and take this peace from Him? Perhaps it's our pride, our need to be better than others, to impress others, to stand out from the crowd. Somehow, we manage to be both insecure, unsure of our own worth, and selfishly arrogant all at the same time! Jesus says to us, however, "Do you want to stand out? Then step down. Be a servant. If you puff yourself up, you'll get the wind knocked out of you. But if you're content to simply be yourself, your life will count for plenty" (Matthew 23:11–12 MSG). In Jesus, we can be truly complete, at peace with ourselves—and then we can use our personal strengths as they were intended to be used.

Remind me, Lord, not to steal my own strength from myself with worry. Make me strong with Your peace.

The Right Opportunity

The Proverbs 31 woman takes advantage of the opportunities that come along. She is able to work with such strength and vigor because she wisely uses all that has been given to her.

The word *opportunity* comes from a Latin word that had to do with the right time, the favorable time, the best time for something to be accomplished. It was also connected to a term ancient sailors used for coming toward a port, blown by favorable winds.

Do we take advantage of the opportunities time brings to us? Inevitably we will miss some, but we can learn to pay better attention. John Maxwell writes, "What are inventors? People who see opportunity in things where others see nothing—people whose senses are alive to creative possibilities." We, too, can practice spotting the "creative possibilities" in our lives!

God is the Creator who has shared portions of His infinite creativity with us. The book of Exodus tells us that God "has filled [us] with the Spirit of God, with skill, with intelligence, with knowledge, and with all craftsmanship, to devise artistic designs" (35:31–32 ESV). Creativity is God's gift to us—and using our creativity is our gift back to God. We are all called to be a part of God's creation, doing our part to enrich the world.

Sometimes, though, we doubt our own powers of creativity, and that self-doubt steals our strength.

Stephen Covey, author of *The 7 Habits of Highly Effective People*, writes:

> The creative process is. . .terrifying. . .because you don't know exactly what's going to happen or where it is going to lead. You don't know what new dangers and challenges you'll find. It takes an enormous amount of internal security to begin with the spirit of adventure, discovery, and creativity. Without doubt, you have to leave the comfort zone of base camp and confront an entirely new and unknown wilderness.[3]

It may seem odd that we could be scared of creativity, but we need to give Stephen Covey's words careful consideration. Are we holding our strength back from the work God wants us to do because we are scared of what we might create? Are we missing opportunities because change makes us uncomfortable—and we don't really want to see the creative possibilities? Inevitably, creativity shakes things up. It brings new things to the world. Management author Edward de Bono writes, "Creativity involves breaking out of established patterns in order to look at things in a different way." Those new perspectives can seem like a threat to our security. Twentieth-century politician James F. Byrnes said, "Too many people are thinking of security, instead of opportunity." And author Mark Twain wrote these words of wisdom: "Twenty years from now you will be more disappointed by the things that you

3. Stephen Covey, *The 7 Habits of Highly Effective People: Powerful Lessons in Personal Change* (New York: Simon & Schuster, 2013).

didn't do than by the ones you did do. So throw off the bowlines. Sail away from the safe harbor. Catch the trade winds in your sails. Explore. Dream. Discover."

Thank You, Creator God, for giving me creativity. Show me the opportunities You are giving me to be creative—and give me the courage and strength to let the wind of Your Spirit fill my sails.

Confident Woman!

The Proverbs 31 woman seems to never doubt her own abilities; she overflows with self-confidence. But surely even she—like all of us—had her moments of self-doubt. And if not, where did she find her strength and confidence? Perhaps she had learned to depend on God for her strength. Her life's experience had taught her that nothing is too hard for the Lord (Genesis 18:14).

Even the Bible's greatest saints had moments when their strength failed them. All of them were weak sometimes. Consider Abraham, who doubted God's ability to give children to him and Sarah. The situation seemed truly hopeless. In fact, giving up hope seemed like the most rational step to take, since both Abraham and Sarah were technically too old to have children. But God asked Abraham to take a look up at the stars and try to count them. Then, with that perspective of endlessness in Abraham's mind, God promised that Abraham and Sarah would have as many descendants as the stars. Currently, there are about 14 million Jews in the world. Clearly God has kept His promise to Abraham. Sometimes we make this promise very spiritual, forgetting exactly what God did for Abraham and Sarah: He gave them sexual and reproductive strength!

The Bible is full of promises God has made to us concerning strength. Again and again, He assures us that even when we are weak, we can be strong in Him. "My flesh and my heart may fail," wrote the psalmist, "but God is the strength of my heart and my portion forever" (Psalm 73:26 NASB). God has the strength to do the impossible in our lives, too. We, too, can lay claim to the promise He made to the apostle Paul: "My grace is sufficient for you, for my power is made perfect in weakness." And we can say with Paul, "Therefore I will boast all the more gladly about my weaknesses, so that Christ's power may rest on me. That is why, for Christ's sake, I delight in weaknesses. . . . For when I am weak, then I am strong" (2 Corinthians 12:9–10 NIV). True strength, Paul tells us, has more to do with love than with force or power. "That you, being rooted and grounded in love," he wrote, "may have strength to comprehend with all the saints what is the breadth and length and height and depth, and to know the love of Christ that surpasses knowledge, that you may be filled with all the fullness of God" (Ephesians 3:17–19 ESV).

And perhaps that is exactly why the Proverbs 31 woman could be so strong: because she was filled with love for God and for her household.

Lord, I acknowledge my weakness today. May it not rob me of my ability to do my work, though. Instead, help me to depend on You for strength. Let Your love flow through me.

A New Outlook

Often, when we feel we lack the strength we need, it's because we're focusing so much on the problem that we can't see anything else. Our enormous difficulty blocks our view, and we can't see opportunities or creative possibilities—or God, who is waiting to lend us His strength.

When that happens, we need to pull away from the situation enough so we can regain our perspective. One of the best ways to gain a new outlook may be to spend some time with scripture. When we turn to the Bible, we find again and again that God helped His people with "His mighty hand and outstretched arm." God's arm is strong, and He is always ready to reach down and lend us a hand!

When we're feeling too weak to handle everything that life is throwing at us, here are some Bible verses to read and ponder.

"Surely the arm of the LORD is not too short to save," said the prophet Isaiah (59:1 NIV), and the prophet Jeremiah affirmed the same message: "Ah, Sovereign LORD, you have made the heavens and the earth by your great power and outstretched arm," said Jeremiah (32:17 NIV). Isaiah also wrote:

> The everlasting God, the LORD, the Creator of the ends of the earth, neither faints nor is weary. His understanding is unsearchable. He gives power to the weak, and to those who have no might He increases strength. Even the youths shall faint and

*be weary, and the young men shall utterly fall,
but those who wait on the L*ORD *shall renew their
strength; they shall mount up with wings like
eagles, they shall run and not be weary, they shall
walk and not faint.* (Isaiah 40:28–31 NKJV)

In the book of Deuteronomy, Joshua told his men before they went into battle, "Be strong and of good courage, do not fear nor be afraid of them; for the LORD your God, He is the One who goes with you. He will not leave you nor forsake you" (31:6 NKJV). And the psalmist gave us these reassuring words:

*I will love You, O L*ORD, *my strength.
The L*ORD *is my rock and my fortress
    and my deliverer;
My God, my strength, in whom I will trust;
My shield and the horn of my salvation,
    my stronghold.
I will call upon the L*ORD, *who is worthy
    to be praised;
So shall I be saved from my enemies.*
    (Psalm 18:1–3 NKJV)

*Lord, please reach down Your strong arm and help me
with this problem that seems so insurmountable.
Give me a new perspective on it. Teach me to rely
on Your strength instead of my own.*

Fitness

The Proverbs 31 woman must have had physical strength as well as spiritual and emotional strength. If we want her to be our model, we need to evaluate our own bodies' fitness. Is this an area of our lives where we need to make changes?

According to many studies, people who exercise regularly are better workers. They perform better at their jobs—in terms of both the quality and quantity of work—and they're happier at work. They have strong arms so they can work vigorously!

Regular exercise makes us stronger in more ways than one. The Mayo Clinic says that people who exercise get sick less, have higher energy levels, sleep better, and have more stable emotions than people who don't. The American Heart Association makes other claims about regular exercise: along with improving heart function and reducing your blood pressure, it improves your physical balance and endurance, and it enhances your self-confidence. People who exercise live longer than people who don't.

So if your daily routines don't involve a lot of physical activity (and many of us have sedentary jobs these days), you might want to consider making exercise a priority in your busy life. It probably seems like you just don't have time to fit in one more thing—but regular exercise will actually make you more productive during your work time.

Your physical strength is also connected to your

diet. Healthy bodies need a balanced diet and good nutrition. They need plenty of vegetables and fruit, as well as whole grains and protein. A steady diet of fast food and processed breads and desserts does *not* build a strong body! Skipping meals because you're too busy to take the time to eat isn't a good idea either. It can make you irritable and light-headed. Your brain chemistry changes when you eat the wrong foods or skip meals, and this will affect your emotions.

At first, changing our habits can be difficult. It requires commitment and discipline. We need to be strongly motivated. Wanting to be thin or fit in order to measure up to our society's standards for feminine beauty may not be enough motivation to keep us focused on caring for our bodies. Instead, we may need to remind ourselves that we are caring for our bodies as a gift to ourselves—and to God.

Our culture often thinks of bodies and souls as separate from each other, but the Bible does not indicate that God sees us that way, and science does not support this perspective either. We can't really separate our bodies' health from our emotional health—and both will intersect with our spiritual health.

God sees the wholeness of our entire being, and He wants us to take care of all aspects of our personhood. We are created in God's image, and as we take care of our bodies, we are also caring for the image of God. We are caring for God's creation. When we do, our spirits will flourish. We will regain the strength that God intended us to have. Like the Proverbs 31 woman, we, too, will be strong and vigorous as we go about our daily work!

God, You know the whole me, mind, soul, and body. You know what I need to be strong. May I be responsible for caring for all aspects of myself so that I may serve You with strength and vigor.

PART VIII

She sees that her trading is profitable,
and her lamp does not go out at night.
—VERSE 18 NIV

A Source Of Light

Here again in verse 18 we find the Proverbs 31 woman proving her wise business practices. She makes sure that her enterprises are "profitable," and she budgets her resources so that she has enough when she needs to rely on them. Metaphorically, we can go still further. If we are like this woman, we will have a source of light even in life's dark times.

That light is our reliance on God and His promises. His Word is powerful—and it's not only found in the Bible. It also lives in our hearts. As God's children, we shine with it, even in the midst of darkness. His life within us leaps up, lighting our way.

And because of this, we don't have to become discouraged or let our hearts be weighed down by pressure and anxiety. Jesus, the True Life, lives in our hearts. We can trust that Life. We can be confident because our light comes from God, and nothing can put it out.

"You will go out in joy and be led forth in peace," said the prophet Isaiah; "the mountains and hills will burst into song before you, and all the trees of the field will clap their hands" (55:12 NIV). Other scriptures affirm the light inside our hearts, the light that will never go out in the night:

> *"If you are filled with light, with no dark corners, then your whole life will be radiant, as though a floodlight were filling you with light."* (Luke 11:36 NLT)

102

For God, who said, "Light shall shine out of darkness," is the One who has shone in our hearts to give the Light of the knowledge of the glory of God in the face of Christ. (2 Corinthians 4:6 NASB)

Jesus. . .said, "I am the light of the world. If you follow me, you won't have to walk in darkness, because you will have the light that leads to life." (John 8:12 NLT)

They that dwell in the land of the shadow of death, upon them hath the light shined. (Isaiah 9:2 KJV)

Lord, I am so grateful that Your light shines in my heart and will never go out!

Next Steps

We have God's light within us—and yet we still run into long spiritual nights where it seems our light has gone out. It could be a long illness that seems to have snuffed it out; it might be a death in the family, the loss of a job, or the breakup of a marriage. Whatever it is, it scares us. It makes us feel as though we can't see the way ahead. We feel as though the light has left us.

When that happens, we may feel as though we are at fault. We wonder if we failed to be as responsible as the Proverbs 31 woman. Was it some carelessness of ours that led to our light going out? Did we do something wrong? Are we lacking in faith?

Author Barbara Brown Taylor wrote in *Time* magazine about this very issue. "Christianity has never had anything nice to say about darkness," she said. "From earliest times, Christians have used 'darkness' as a synonym for sin, ignorance, spiritual blindness, and death." But, she said, God is in the darkness.

> *When, despite all my best efforts, the lights have gone off in my life. . .plunging me into the kind of darkness that turns my knees to water, nonetheless . . .I have learned things in the dark that I could never have learned in the light, things that have saved my life over and over again, so that there is really only one logical conclusion. I need darkness as much as I need light.*[4]

---

4. Barbara Brown Taylor, "In Praise of Darkness," *Time*, April 17, 2014, http://time.com/65543/barbara-brown-taylor-in-praise-of-darkness.

It helps to know that these dark times come to everyone. They are normal. They are even healthy. Just as the natural world needs both day and night, so we, too, need periods of spiritual illumination and times of spiritual obscurity. But knowing that doesn't take away the fear and pain we experience during these dark times.

Sometimes it seems as though we cannot make it through one more day, let alone another night when we lie awake worrying. Struggles, hardships, pain, and difficulty envelop us. We cry out (to God, to life), "Please. No more! I can't endure anything else."

In those desperate moments, we need to ask ourselves: "Can you make it through the next hour?" If so, we can put our energy into that—and nothing more. If we can't make it through the next hour, can we endure the next half hour. . .the next fifteen minutes. . .the next minute? Then we can commit ourselves to that small space of time and look no further ahead.

Sometimes God's light only lights the darkness one step ahead. In that case, we need to simply take that single step. We don't need to worry about the next step (or the next minute, the next hour, the next day). As we take moments, minutes, hours as they come, one at a time, not worrying about the darkness that seems to lie ahead, we will find that God gives us the light we need. Slowly, moment by moment, we move into a new place. A new day dawns.

Author Oswald Chambers wrote, "Dark times are allowed and come to us through the sovereignty of God. Are we prepared to let God do what He wants with us? Are we prepared to be separated from the outward, evident blessings of God?"

During dark times, Lord, increase my faith in You. May I be willing to walk a step at a time. Help me to be willing to learn whatever You are trying to teach me during this dark period in my life.

Preparedness

Many things can cause our spiritual and emotional nights. Plans we were counting on fall apart. Our dreams are put to death. Our hearts break. Life steals from us the very things we think we need most. Unfortunately, that's life!

If we are like the Proverbs 31 woman, we will expect the dark times—and prepare for them. One way to do this is by building good habits during the "daylight." In other words, we create routines during easier days that will carry us through the hard times. This might mean spending time alone with God every day. Or it could mean making exercise as routine as brushing our teeth. Habitual routines can carry us along even when we have no energy to spare—and these healthy habits will give us the strength we need in the darkness.

Good habits don't always have to be things we *do*; they can also be habits of thinking. The "Jesus Prayer" is a good example of this. For centuries, some Christians have mentally repeated this prayer—"Lord Jesus Christ, Son of the living God, have mercy on me, a sinner"—until it wears a mental groove in their thoughts. This is not vain repetition but a training of their minds' habits. Their mental default is always a prayer that reminds them of their relationship with God.

Often we have negative mental habits, and these can become even more destructive during our lives' dark times. We might have a habit of criticizing ourselves inside our heads—for example, telling ourselves things like this: "You are so stupid"; "You're looking silly"; "You look fat"; or "You'll never be able to do that." We become so accustomed to this silent, habitual stream of inner conversation that we may not even be aware of what we're doing. All that negative self-talk becomes particularly deadly when we're already tired or anxious. It can paralyze us so that we can't find our way out of the darkness.

Psychologists suggest that we create habitual patterns of positive self-talk during our up times so that those habits will make us stronger during the down times. This doesn't mean we tell ourselves things we know to be untrue; we don't need to say, "You're drop-dead gorgeous. You're a goddess," for example, if that's not quite the truth. Instead, we can make a habit of mentally affirming ourselves, as well as God's power to help us grow. We might say things like, "I know I'm overweight right now, but God can help me lose ten pounds," or "I blew that opportunity, but I'll learn from my mistake, and with God's help, I'll do better next time."

The first step, though, is to become aware of the bad habits we have in place that will only plunge us deeper into confusion during the nighttimes of our lives—and then we can take steps to replace them with habits that will give us strength. Then we, like the Proverbs 31 woman, will be able to work profitably, to God's glory, even in the darkness.

God, shine Your light on the habits I have in place that confuse me and darken my understanding. Reveal them to me clearly so that I can replace them with positive habits that will help me navigate even the darkest nights.

℘Prayer ℒife

The woman described in Proverbs 31 engages in "profitable" activities. The literal meaning of the Hebrew words used in this verse is this: "She senses that what she gains from her work is pleasing." In other words, she takes pleasure in it, but it's not a selfish, ego-stroking kind of pleasure. Instead, it's the joy that comes from knowing the work you're doing is good for you and for the world around you.

In fact, our work should have something in common with prayer. C. S. Lewis wrote that the two ways by "which we are allowed to produce events may be called work and prayer." The fifth-century Christian Benedict of Nursia taught something very similar. His motto was, "Pray and work," and he believed that prayer and work should be partners, one taking place internally while the other occurs externally, like two hands working together.

Here are some suggestions for merging your prayer life with your work life into a unified whole:

- Start each morning by thanking God for the job you have. Ask His help in adopting the attitude recommended in Colossians 3:23: "Work willingly at whatever you do, as though you were working for the Lord rather than for people" (NLT).

- If you have a morning commute, by car or train, use the time as an opportunity to pray for the day ahead. If you have headphones and a smartphone, you might want to use a site like Pray as You Go (http://www.pray-as-you-go.org/home), which gives you daily devotions that consist of music, scripture, meditation, and prayer.

- If you work at a computer, use the time as it turns on to dedicate all that you do on it to God.
- Before a meeting with coworkers, customers, or supervisors, ask God to guide your words and give you insight.
- Whenever you receive or send an e-mail, or when you make or receive a phone call, get in the habit of silently blessing the person with whom you are communicating. (A blessing can be as fast and as simple as "Bless you," or "God, please bless _____.")
- Also make a habit of silently blessing your coworkers and supervisors (even the ones who are hard to like) each time you pass them in the hall or walk by their offices.
- Never gossip about your coworkers!
- On payday, thank God for His financial provision—and ask Him to bless the company or person for whom you work.
- As you leave your workplace and go home, thank God for being with you throughout the day. Ask Him to help you to mentally disengage from your work so you can relax and focus on your family.

Be the Lord of my work, I pray. May my work be a prayer, so that it may please You even as it pleases my own heart.

The Most Joy

Sometimes we need to take a moment so that we can perceive what truly *does* give us the most joy. Our society tells us that we need money to be happy. Advertisements and commercials fill our brains with the idea that we need to buy, buy, buy in order to be content. Magazines and movies make us think we need to look a certain way to be happy with ourselves. We need to readjust our perceptions so that we, like the Proverbs 31 woman, can sense what truly gives our hearts joy. We need to have a better understanding of what is truly profitable for us.

Paul wrote to Timothy, "True godliness with contentment is itself great wealth" (1 Timothy 6:6 NLT). Jesus taught that we are to seek God and His righteousness as our first priority (Matthew 6:33). This is the first step toward realigning our values with what is *truly* real. Like Paul, we need to learn to be content no matter our circumstances (Philippians 4:11–13), trusting that God is always caring for our needs. Perhaps the best thing we can do to be sure we are looking at work and wealth from God's perspective is to read often these words of Jesus:

> *"Do not store up for yourselves treasures on earth, where moths and vermin destroy, and where thieves break in and steal. But store up for yourselves treasures in heaven, where moths and vermin do not destroy, and where thieves do not break in and steal. For where your treasure is, there your heart will be also. . . . You cannot serve both God and money.*

"Therefore I tell you, do not worry about your life, what you will eat or drink; or about your body, what you will wear. Is not life more than food, and the body more than clothes? Look at the birds of the air; they do not sow or reap or store away in barns, and yet your heavenly Father feeds them. Are you not much more valuable than they? Can any one of you by worrying add a single hour to your life?

"And why do you worry about clothes? See how the flowers of the field grow. They do not labor or spin. Yet I tell you that not even Solomon in all his splendor was dressed like one of these. If that is how God clothes the grass of the field, which is here today and tomorrow is thrown into the fire, will he not much more clothe you—you of little faith? So do not worry, saying, 'What shall we eat?' or 'What shall we drink?' or 'What shall we wear?' For. . .your heavenly Father knows that you need them. But seek first his kingdom and his righteousness, and all these things will be given to you as well. Therefore do not worry about tomorrow, for tomorrow will worry about itself."
(Matthew 6:19–21, 24–34 NIV)

In the Gospel of Mark, Jesus asked, "What does it profit a man to gain the whole world, and forfeit his soul?" (8:36 NASB). We need to keep that always in mind, even—or maybe especially—in the midst of our busy lives!

Jesus, You understand how humans think. You know how easily we worry. Help me to look at life from Your perspective. Remind me to listen to Your words rather than the messages the world gives me. May I understand what is truly profitable for me.

All We Need

As we read the Gospels, we see over and over again examples of Jesus' ability to provide us with all we need. Often He turned hopeless situations into opportunities for creative possibility.

When the disciples needed to feed a crowd of people, Jesus multiplied a little boy's bread and fishes, so that somehow a tiny meal became large enough to feed thousands. When the disciples needed to pay the taxes, Jesus told them to go catch a fish—which would have the money they needed in its mouth. When the disciples had fished all night and caught nothing, Jesus directed them to throw their net again on the other side of the boat. When they did, their net was so full of fish that it was too heavy for them to haul it on board.

All these stories teach us that Jesus was able again and again to take care of His followers' needs. He didn't do it by giving them great financial wealth. Instead, He worked with the ordinary materials of daily life to create abundance in their lives.

Jesus depended on His Father to supply His needs—and like Jesus, we, too, are God's children. God is a loving Parent who takes joy in giving to us. In Matthew 7:11, Jesus reminds us, "If you. . .know how to give good gifts to your children, how much more will your Father in heaven give good gifts to those who ask him!" (NIV). Like the Proverbs 31 woman, we, too, can perceive the true wealth in our lives. If we let Him, God will show us the coins hidden in unexpected places, the fish waiting to be caught, and the food ready to be multiplied.

God's providence is big enough to encompass all of creation. From the beginning of the universe to its end; from the animate world of all living creatures to the inanimate world of chemicals, electricity, and gravity; from seconds of time to eons; from birth to death; from joy to sadness—each and every thing is held within the shelter of God's love.

If God can do all that, then He is certainly big enough to handle our needs!

Creator God, Your providence encompasses my life.
May I learn to trust You ever more completely.
Overcome my doubt that puts limits on Your love.
Teach me to expect You to do amazing things in my life.
Give me an expectation of blessing, and help me
to see what I need most to be truly rich.

PART IX

In her hand she holds the distaff
and grasps the spindle with her fingers.
—VERSE 19 NIV

Strength And Intelligence

The woman depicted in Proverbs 31 is talented and competent. Her tasks are quite different from ours (most of us probably haven't held a distaff or grasped a spindle recently), but she juggles every bit as many responsibilities as we do in the twenty-first century. In fact, we may be a little intimidated by the strength and dignity that clothe her. She is able to accomplish so *much*, from caring for her husband to planting vineyards, from undertaking business affairs to providing food for her household. And she seems to do it all so seamlessly!

Meanwhile, as we try to manage our own responsibilities, we may feel pulled in countless conflicting directions. We need to meet a deadline at work—and get supper on the table. We need to get ourselves to work on time—and our children to school before the bell rings. We need to do the laundry—and volunteer at school. Our lives don't seem very seamless! Living up to the standards of the Proverbs 31 woman can seem impossible.

But the author's point was not to shame women by holding up an impossible paragon of virtue for them to emulate. Instead, the writer is taking "women's work" seriously; the author is honoring the strength and intelligence needed to run a household while at the same time being a businesswoman.

Meanwhile, our culture has taught us to see housework as menial and demeaning. We dismiss it as not "real work," the sort of work we get paid for doing. Our world often thinks of household labor as the jobs people don't get paid all that much for doing. It's "servants' work" (which is a far different thing from feeling like you are *of service*). Preparing food and caring for a family are often undervalued, despite how essential they are for life.

Housework *is* menial—but the original Latin word from which our modern word comes had nothing to do with inferiority. Instead, it meant "to remain, to dwell." When we do this sort of work, we are not just taking care of inanimate objects; we are creating a home, a place where our families (and ourselves) can get a taste of the stability and permanence of God, "with whom is no variableness, neither shadow of turning" (James 1:17 KJV).

Psalm 123:2 tells us: "Consider this: as the eyes of a. . .female servant focus on what her mistress provides, so our eyes focus on the LORD our God, until he has mercy on us" (ISV). This verse puts God in the role of a housewife, the mistress of a household. Here God is the one who manages a complicated household; like the woman in Proverbs 31, God provides nourishment for us, clothes us, and opens loving arms to us. God watches over our affairs and is intimately involved in the physical details of our lives.

So why do we resent doing the same sort of work for our families?

May my hands be Your hands, Lord, as I do my work, both in my home and in my workplace. May my small efforts reflect Your greater work. Use me. Live in me.

For The Lord

In the book of Ephesians, Paul advises us: "Work with enthusiasm, as though you were working for the Lord rather than for people" (6:7 NLT).

Sometimes it's hard to feel like we're working for the Lord when we're busy sweeping floors and changing babies' diapers, grocery shopping and paying bills. As we do these ordinary tasks, however, we can choose to consciously sanctify them by giving each thing to God.

Like spinning thread with a distaff and a spindle, the cycle of our days goes round and round. We do the same jobs again and again and again. We struggle to be patient as we pick up our husbands' dirty socks from the bedroom floor for the fifth time this week. We wipe up spilled juice from the kitchen floor today, just like we did yesterday and the day before. We answer our children's questions over and over. We make the same drive to work each day; it's so familiar that most of the time we drive it on autopilot.

But each of these seemingly small and even meaningless tasks gains a sense of purpose when we begin to do them for the Lord.

It's not always easy. Sometimes we may need to rely on our powers of imagination. Children are good at make-believe, but as adults we may have neglected this mental skill. It's a useful one, though, and one that God can use and bless. The next time you're doing a tedious chore, your imagination may help you catch a glimpse of what's truly real. As you scrub the kitchen floor, imagine that Jesus will walk across it; as you prepare a report at work, imagine that Jesus will review it; as you do the family laundry, imagine that Jesus will wear the clean clothes. This is not merely a make-believe game; when we offer each thing we do as service to Jesus, even the smallest, most mundane task becomes holy.

We might also try praying as we work, using the rhythm of washing dishes, sweeping floors, or stopping at traffic lights as opportunities to structure short prayers. For example, we might pray for a different member of the family at each red light we come to. Or we could pray these lines from the Psalms as we push the vacuum cleaner back and forth: "May the favor of the Lord our God rest on us; establish the work of our hands for us—yes, establish the work of our hands" (90:17 NIV). As we create these habits of prayer, we will be able to practice Paul's advice: "Always work enthusiastically for the Lord, for you know that nothing you do for the Lord is ever useless" (1 Corinthians 15:58 NLT).

Dear Lord, sanctify the repetitive chores that fill my day with Your presence. May Your grace and love be woven through my work. I offer each task to You.

For His Glory

As we care for our homes and families, we are also participating in the work of God's providence. In the words of author Douglas J. Schuurman, we are given the opportunity to "participate in God's provident care for creation through [our] activities."

Often, however, we fall into the habit of thinking of "church work" and "worldly work," as though one were somehow holier than the other. R. C. Sproul Jr. said: "Our tendency in the evangelical church is to separate our spiritual life from our ordinary life. If we can have the perspective that we're working for the kingdom and we're working for Jesus and that our work is a sacrifice to Him, we end up richly rewarded."[5]

Martin Luther, the great Protestant reformer, agreed. He felt that preaching and doing ordinary work, when performed in faith, with integrity and love, were equally as valuable. When a shoemaker in Luther's community was converted and began to follow Christ, he came to Luther and asked him, "Now that I'm a Christian, what should I do?" He was actually hoping he could leave behind all his possessions and responsibilities and take on a job in the church.

Luther's answer took the man by surprise. "Make a good shoe," Luther said simply, "and sell it at a fair price." That was the work God had given to this

---

5. Lee Webb, "Why Work Matters to God," CBN *News*. http://www.cbn.com/cbnnews/us/2013/September/Labor-Day-Why-Work-Matters-to-God.

particular man—and it was as valuable to the world as preaching and acts of charity. After all, where would we be if all the shoemakers stopped making shoes and became preachers!

Solomon's advice in Ecclesiastes 9:10 is very similar to Luther's: "Whatever you do, do well" (NLT). Again and again, scripture teaches us that our work *matters*. When the woman in Proverbs picked up her spindle and distaff, she wasn't engaging in mere busywork; she was making something useful, something that could be used by her household or by those in her community. In *The Purpose-Driven Life*, Rick Warren wrote, "God designed you to make a difference with your life. . . . You were created to *add* to life on earth, not just take from it. God wants you to give something back. This is God's. . .purpose for your life."[6] Like the Proverbs 31 woman, we are each called to work diligently—and in the process, we enrich the world for others and give glory to God.

The great preacher Charles Spurgeon believed that faith can lead us to serve God in our "daily calling." He wrote, "Never is life more ennobled than when we do all things as unto God. This makes drudgery sublime, and links the poorest servant with the brightest angel. Seraphs serve God in heaven, and you and I may serve him in. . .the kitchen, and be as accepted as they are . . .endeavoring to order everything according to the rules of love to God and love to men."[7]

---

6. Rick Warren, *The Purpose-Driven Life: What on Earth Am I Here For?* (Grand Rapids: Zondervan, 2012).

7. Charles Spurgeon, *The Complete Works of Charles Spurgeon*, volume 27 (Harrington, DE: Delmarva, 2013).

Lord, as I go about my work, may I remember that the angels in heaven are also working for Your glory— and I am working alongside them. You value my small efforts as much as theirs!

God Goes Ahead

Before Jesus went to the cross, He prayed to His Father, "I have glorified You on the earth. I have finished the work You have given me to do" (John 17:4 NKJV). We need the same commitment and dedication Jesus had to the work He was called to.

Jeremiah compares God to a potter who has created each of us for a specific purpose and continually shapes us (18:4). The implication here is that this is an ongoing process. God asks you to do one job today—but tomorrow you may find that all the while He was shaping you to do something different. The loss of a job or a failed career can be a blow to our very identities—but we need to trust that God will use these circumstances. What seems like failure may in fact be the training ground for a new work He wants you to accomplish.

As humans, we live in time, unable to see the future. The good news is that God always goes ahead of us (Isaiah 52:12; Psalm 139:5). We need not fear the hands of the potter who is shaping our lives, for God's care is ongoing. It never ends.

Secure in that knowledge, we don't need to compare our work to others' or try to compete. I doubt that the Proverbs 31 woman cared how fast or skillfully her sisters could use the distaff and spindle compared to her; she was focused on her own work. Paul wrote to the Galatians, "Everyone should look at himself and see how he does his own work. Then he can be happy in what he has done. He should not compare himself with his neighbor" (6:4 NLV).

When your coworker gets a promotion, don't worry and feel diminished because you didn't. If you realize your neighbor's house is tidier than yours, don't feel that you're not as good as she is. Instead, be willing to be clay in God's hands, trusting that He is working through your work, leading you into new opportunities, even in the midst of what may seem like failure.

Each day, commit your work to God. Do the work that is at hand, that needs to be done—and seek His direction for the future. God never stops opening new doors for us, just as He did for the apostle Paul (1 Corinthians 16:9; 2 Corinthians 2:12; Colossians 4:3). He has an ongoing purpose for our lives.

Viktor Frankl wrote: "Everyone has his own specific vocation or mission in life; everyone must carry out a concrete assignment that demands fulfillment. Therein he cannot be replaced, nor can his life be repeated, thus, everyone's task is unique as his specific opportunity to implement it."[8] Right now, God is shaping you for the specific opportunities that lie ahead.

Lord, use today's work to prepare me
for tomorrow's service to You.

---

8. Victor Frankl, *Man's Search for Meaning.* (Boston: Beacon Press, 2006).

A Gift To Be Received

No matter what the Proverbs 31 woman was doing—and she did a lot!—she seems always to have had a sense of her larger vocation. The word *vocation* comes from the Latin for "voice." Vocation is that still, small voice that calls to us in countless different ways. The only way to follow it is to first listen for it.

We often think of our work as being all about achieving goals, and we may think a vocation is something to be achieved. We think of it as a voice calling to us from the world around us, asking us to go further, do better, achieve more.

Instead, however, a vocation is most truly a gift to be received from God's hands. Hidden within this gift, we find a deeper understanding of our own identities, the individuals God created us to be. The voice that is calling to us turns out to be God's, speaking to us from within our own hearts.

Accepting our vocations as gifts doesn't take away the need to work hard. But it does mean we need to give up working so hard to be someone or something we weren't meant to be. An old Jewish story tells about Rabbi Zusya, who said, "When I die, God will not ask me, 'Why were you not Moses?' He will ask me, 'Why were you not Zusya?'"

When we answer the "Who am I?" question as honestly as we can, we will be more authentically connected to the community around us and will serve more faithfully the people whose lives we touch. Ultimately, the gift of ourselves is the only gift we have to give.

Sometimes we all manage to lose track of our true selves. We find ourselves trapped in work that seems to stifle our creativity. We don't merely feel bored at work; we feel deeply unhappy. We long to be doing something different.

When that happens, we should listen to what our hearts are telling us. We don't always pay attention to our own feelings and intuitions, though. We often treat them with distrust instead of respect. But God can use our emotional reactions to guide us to the work He wants for us, the work where we can blossom and grow into the authentic people we are called to be.

The Quaker author Douglas Steere wrote that the question we all ask sooner or later, "Who am I?" will always lead us to the equally important question, "Whose am I?" We cannot discover our true selves separate from our relationship with God.

Lord, help me to discover my true self as I do the work for which You have called me—and in doing that work, may I give myself more completely to You.

Other Possibilities?

Do you think the Proverbs 31 woman ever felt restless as she held her distaff? While her spindle turned around and around, did she daydream about other possibilities? Did she wonder if there were new skills she could learn, new opportunities she might pursue? Did she question whether the meaning of her vocation might be changing?

If you're feeling restless with your work, here are some things to keep in mind:

- Right now, deal with your current work. Trust that God is shaping you for the future a little at a time. Meanwhile, what you do today matters to His kingdom.

- When odd and unexpected opportunities pop up, don't automatically say no because you've never done anything similar. Remember that opportunities are moments of creative possibility—and God may use them to open new doors in your life.

- Don't try to follow someone else's dream. Your parents may have hoped you would become a lawyer. Your best friend may be positive you'd make a perfect teacher. Your current supervisor may be grooming you for another position in the company. Don't let any of this drown out the little voice inside you that may be calling you in a different direction. Remember, God often speaks to us through the deepest, truest desires of our hearts.

- Notice the things you are good at. Make a list of talents you have that you're not getting a chance to use in your current job. Be open to new opportunities that will allow you to explore these strengths.

- Don't worry about being "the best"; don't keep score. The true desire of your heart is never going to insist that you beat the competition; instead, it will lead you to your own unique mission.

- Be willing to change course. You may have spent a lot of time and money on getting educated for a specific career—only to discover that you feel led to something completely different. Trust God. He may want to use your education and training in ways you could never have anticipated.

- Most of all, rest in God's love. Know that He will give you guidance at exactly the right moment—and probably not a moment sooner!

Loving God, lead me to the work You want me to do next. I trust myself to Your love and guidance.

Vehicles Of Prayer And Service

Author Paul Bosch wrote, "Whatever you do repeatedly has the power to shape you, has the power to make you over into a different person—even if you're not totally 'engaged' in every minute." Spinning thread with a distaff and a spindle might be considered the sort of work that's not all that engaging. While our Proverbs 31 woman's hands were busy, her mind was free to wander. And yet at the same time, the repetitive work of her hands was shaping her, maybe even in ways she didn't fully realize. The discipline and structure of this manual labor created a space for her mind to grow and stretch, for her spirit to be refreshed, and for her imagination to be challenged. It hollowed out a place where she could meet God.

We, too, can find that our daily, manual tasks shape us in positive ways as we allow ourselves to be changed and shaped by their patterns. In the midst of laundry and meal preparation, we can hear God's voice. We find that love is having its way with us. We discover that we are slowly being changed into the people He always intended us to be.

Brother Lawrence, author of *The Practice of the Presence of God*, made this same discovery. He wrote:

> O my God, since You are with me, and I must now, in obedience to You, apply my attention to these outward tasks, I ask that You give me the grace to continue in Your presence. With that goal in mind,

prosper my efforts with Your help. Receive everything I do as a gift to You. Possess all my love." [9]

On another occasion, Brother Lawrence also wrote, "We ought not to be weary of doing little things for the love of God, who regards not the greatness of the work, but the love with which it is performed."

Work is an essential and important part of human life. Some work gives us opportunities to express our creativity. All work can be a vehicle of prayer and service to God, as well as love to our families and communities. Work helps us to discover the people God created us to be. But ultimately, we are not defined by our work. Our souls are bigger than the jobs we do. The work of the Proverbs 31 woman was vital and life-giving—but her personhood spread wider than all those vineyards and spindles and fields. It was a grander and deeper thing than her many achievements.

So as we go about our daily work—both the seemingly mindless tasks and the tasks that seem so big and important to us—we give ourselves to its repetition; we yield ourselves to the structure and demands that life places on us, and we find within that framework a way to serve God. And at the same time, we know that we are not loved *because* of our work. It is an expression of our love for God, but His love flows to us in the beating of our hearts, in our very breath. He loves us because we simply *are*.

9. Ellyn Sanna, *Brother Lawrence: Christian Zen Master* (Vestal, NY: Anamchara Books, 2011).

I pray, dear God, that You would use my work to shape me. Come to me while my hands are busy with the same tasks they have done so many times. Thank You that when I can no longer work, You will still love me as much as ever. Even if I can no longer think and pray the way I do now, even if I can only sit in a rocking chair and stare into space, Your love will be unchanged. Your love will continue to come to me even then.

PART X

*She opens her arms to the poor
and extends her hands to the needy.*
—VERSE 20 NIV

Reaching Out

Our Proverbs 31 woman is not focused only on the concerns of her own household and businesses; she also reaches out to those in the community who are in need. She is a perfect example of someone who uses her wealth as it was intended to be used, a current that flows freely both in and out, with the same healthy movement of the body's breath and blood.

The apostle Paul expressed this free flow of resources into our lives and then out again to others with a different metaphor. He wrote, "Remember this: Whoever sows sparingly will also reap sparingly, and whoever sows generously will also reap generously" (2 Corinthians 9:6 NIV).

God's grace and provision flow through a web of relationships. Selfishness is like plaque clogging the arteries in this circulation. If we don't allow His blessings to flow freely through us to others, then we will no longer be able to receive them either.

It's not always easy to open our hearts and reach out our hands to others. Our natural impulse is to keep things for ourselves and the people who are closest to us. After living in a me-first world all our lives, this outlook seems to just make sense. We feel that giving away our resources might put our own households at risk.

But Paul continues in 2 Corinthians, "Each of you should give what you have decided in your heart to give, not reluctantly or under compulsion, for God loves a cheerful giver. And God is able to bless you abundantly, so that in all things at all times, having all that you need, you will abound in every good work" (9:7–8 NIV).

We try to put boundary lines around this divine claim on our wealth. "God expects us to be reasonable," we tell ourselves. "We can't just give everything away, can we?"

But just as we are not to put boundaries on our love for our husbands, we cannot set limits on the love we show to others. Christ's love made Him completely vulnerable—to the point that He gave everything He had, even His life—and we are called to follow Him, to live like He did, to love like He did.

When we are afraid to give beyond what's comfortable, we are not relying on God's bounty to provide for our needs. We are assuming we are living in a world where there are just not enough resources to go around for everyone, and we want to hold on to the piece we've staked our claim to. But the reality is this: we live in a world that's rich with God's blessings. Those blessings come in many shapes and forms; sometimes they may come to us in the form of monetary wealth, but other times God will show us His infinite abundance in other ways.

As long as we place our trust only in our own abilities—no matter how great they may be— God's grace remains something we've never truly experienced. But once we begin to give from hearts that have opened wide, beyond the line of what is safe, then the grace of God comes alive in our lives. We do not need to fear we will not have enough, for we are a part of a body where circulation is healthy. When we allow life to flow out of us to others, we can be certain it will flow into us, replacing what we have given. "Out of his fullness we have all received grace in place of grace already given" (John 1:16 NIV).

Generous Lord, thank You for all You have given me. May I never clog the flow of Your love. Make me a healthy artery in Your body. Use me to bring love and blessing to others.

Multiplied Efforts

The Proverbs 31 woman was confident in God's ability to multiply her efforts. She could give freely, with no sense of lack. She knew there would always be enough to go around. We, too, can have this same confidence. What's more, we have the benefit of something our woman didn't: we have the example of Jesus. We have the stories told in the Gospels about His life to show us just how tangible God's abundance can be.

Think about that day out on the hillside when Jesus fed the five thousand. The disciples and the crowd who were gathered around them must have thought Jesus had lost His mind as He began to tear the small loaves and fish into pieces. How could such a tiny amount of food do them any good? But something amazing happened. As Jesus and the disciples passed out the bread and fish, there was plenty for each and every member of those five thousand families. Jesus didn't give them just a snack, something to tide them over until they could go home and get something better to eat. No, the people all ate until they were full. And then the disciples collected the leftovers.

But this miracle wouldn't have happened if a boy hadn't been willing to share the little he had. We, too, are called to share, but we don't always have the boy's openhearted willingness. The problem is we never seem to have enough of anything for ourselves.

No matter what our financial circumstances, no matter how big or how little our paychecks, we all worry about money. And money's not the only thing we lack. We also bemoan our small supplies of energy . . .and patience. . .and creativity. . .and living space. Most of all, none of us has enough time. We perceive that our lives are filled with lack and need—so when we're asked to share with others, we often hold on tight to what little we have. After all, in so many areas of our lives we genuinely feel poverty stricken. How can we share when our own hands are so empty?

But Jesus doesn't ask us to share only those things of which we have plenty. Instead, He asks that we simply take whatever we *do* have, no matter how small and limited, and place it all in His hands. Common sense may tell us there won't be enough to go around, but that doesn't matter; Jesus will multiply our meager morsels of money—and time, energy, and talent. He will see that there's enough for everyone—including ourselves—with more left over.

All we have to do is offer our hearts and lives to Christ. It doesn't matter if what we have is perfect or plentiful; what matters is that we give it to Him. Like the little boy who gave Jesus his bread and fish, we will be amazed by the bounty of Christ's grace.

Jesus, help me to have the strength to give everything I have. It seems so little, so insignificant. It doesn't seem like it's enough for me, so how can it be enough to do the world any good? I put it in Your hands anyway. Multiply it to Your glory. Use it to feed the world.

Honest With God

We shouldn't beat ourselves up if giving doesn't come easily to us. The pain of learning to give is good for our souls. God teaches us through it, and we learn more about our own natures as well as God's.

Like everything else we do, giving usually gets easier with practice. Each time we see that God will truly take care of us, we gain more confidence in His providence. We are able to give more confidently. But that very confidence based on past experience means that our giving may not mean as much as it does in the beginning, when giving asks us to simply let go and blindly trust, not knowing for sure what will happen.

We don't have to pretend that this is anything but hard. We can be honest with God—and with ourselves—about our fears. Sometimes it may help us to express our feelings out loud in prayer. We might even write them down in a letter to our Lord.

Here's a letter I wrote on an occasion when I felt God was asking more of me than I knew how to give:

> *Dear Lord,*
>
> *You ask me to give You everything. But I have so little to offer.*
>
> *I've always put my confidence in my own skills and abilities. Now I've reached the end of my strength. My talent and determination have let me down; I'm exhausted and discouraged. I just don't have the energy to keep trying.*

I don't have much to give right now, Lord. All I can give You today is my weariness, my loss of hope, my failures. They don't seem like appropriate gifts for the Creator of the universe.

I've been holding tight to these pitiful possessions, though. Now I give them to You. I can't imagine what good they will do—but if You could feed five thousand from one small lunch, then I'll trust You to use even my life's broken fragments.

Now I'll wait for Your grace, Lord. Surprise me.

After I wrote this note, I felt God's silent, wordless answer in my heart. If I could have put it in words, it would have been something like this:

My dear child, your heart is beating with My love; open it to others. Be willing to let it break so that there is nothing left to stop the flow of My life through you.

I have entrusted you with gifts and talents; use them now for Me. I have plans for them. They will bless others richly.

Don't be afraid, dear child. I will go with you and ahead of you each step of the way. Take courage. Step out into the unknown. I'm big enough to handle whatever happens.

Lord, You know how hard it is for me to give away the little I have. Give me the strength to let go and trust You.

Clothed In Compassion

In his letter to the Colossians, Paul wrote, "Therefore, as God's chosen people, holy and dearly loved, clothe yourselves with compassion, kindness, humility, gentleness and patience" (3:12 NIV). The Proverbs 31 woman is a good model of someone who clothed herself with compassion and kindness.

Compassion isn't the same thing as pity. Pity is just a feeling, but compassion takes action. Merriam-Webster's Dictionary defines compassion as "sympathetic consciousness of others' distress together with a desire to alleviate it." God gives us the perfect example of compassion because He sent His Son, a part of His very Self, to die for us (John 3:16). And now He wants to clothe us with that same compassion.

The Greek words in Colossians 3:12 mean literally, "Let your heart—your emotions, the inner center of your being—be turned into a garment of love." No matter what our emotions tell us (no matter how much selfishness or fear or resentment we *feel* inside), we need to persistently get up each morning and wrap these new clothes tight around our hearts. Eventually we may be able to put them on as automatically as we step into our underwear—but at first, it will take effort and discipline.

We may already have tender hearts. The sight of suffering may make us hurt inside. We may wince when we see the faces on television of those who are starving and in pain. But our tender hearts will do those people little good if we don't take action. We often feel we are too far away or too powerless to help. The world's problems seem overwhelming.

But no one is asking us to solve the entire world's problems; we are asked only to do our small part.

We need to take a sharp-eyed, objective look at our lives. Are we truly clothed in the compassion of God's love? Do we notice the need in our own communities? Are we reaching out in love to everyone with whom we come into contact? Are we prayerfully and thoughtfully considering how our resources of money, time, and talent should be used to help others?

As we begin to wear God's garment, prayer is the first step to take. Through prayer we can reach around the world with heavenly power. Prayer transcends time and space. It can reach from our hearts to starving children in Africa, to a homeless woman on a city street, and to a man dying of AIDS in India.

Clothe me in Your compassion, loving Lord. Use my hands, my money, my heart to bless others who are in need.

Rebuilding Walls

Compassion begins with prayer, but it doesn't stop there. The Proverbs 31 woman reached out to those in need in practical, concrete ways. "Praying to make a difference is unselfish praying," John Hull wrote, "[and] in all likelihood is going to cost us something. It's probably going to make us uncomfortable and take us to places—spiritually and geographically—where we wouldn't dare go unless God had birthed it in our hearts. . . . Praying to make a difference in this world means we learn to get past ourselves and our problems and pursue a greater purpose."[10]

Often we would rather change the television channel when some scene of distant suffering comes on our screens. We feel powerless to help, so we'd rather not even think about it. We'd rather pretend it didn't exist. In the Old Testament, however, Nehemiah gives us an example of an unselfish man of prayer who had the courage to look beyond the boundaries of his own immediate existence. He didn't bury his head in the sand so that he wouldn't have to face the fact that distant people were suffering.

Nehemiah was a Jew living in Persia, where he served the king of that land. Jerusalem was a long way away, but when Nehemiah's brother came back from the land of Judah, Nehemiah asked him for news of the Jews in Jerusalem. Nehemiah discovered that the people there were in a desperate situation. The wall

10. John Hull, *Pivotal Praying: Connecting to God in Times of Great Need* (Nashville: Thomas Nelson, 2002).

of Jerusalem was broken, leaving the Jews defenseless against their enemies (Nehemiah 1:1–3).

As soon as he heard about this situation, Nehemiah was overcome with emotion. His sympathy for the people in Jerusalem was so great that he felt it as though their pain was his own. He sat down and began to cry. We, too, might have gone this far if we had heard about people who were suffering far away— but after we were done crying, we probably would have wiped our eyes, put the whole thing out of our minds, and returned to our own lives. Nehemiah went another step, though; the Bible says he fasted and prayed (Nehemiah 1:4–11). He gave his heart to the situation, and he did not stop giving, even though there was little he could do as yet.

Nehemiah's prayer may not have changed the situation in Jerusalem—not yet. But it changed Nehemiah, in ways that were probably painful. As he went about his duties for the king, the king noticed the sadness in his face. Nehemiah had already built a reputation of integrity and hard work, and the king trusted and liked him, so the king asked Nehemiah what was troubling him.

Now Nehemiah had an opportunity to do more than pray. He told someone else about what was happening in Jerusalem. And from there he took even greater action. He asked for permission to return to Jerusalem and do whatever he could to help the city rebuild its wall. Jerusalem probably had many problems, but Nehemiah didn't try to tackle them all. Instead, he focused on a specific problem where he felt he could make a difference. And then he depended on God's help for the outcome. "The God of heaven will give us success," he told the people who were skeptical about what he was doing (Nehemiah 2:20 NIV).

What walls can we help rebuild?

Dear God, show me the places where I can make a difference. Direct me to the specific situations where You need me to open my heart and my hands.

A Reciprocal Nature

In Genesis, God promises Abraham, "I will bless you. . .and you will be a blessing to others" (12:2 NLT). Here again we see the reciprocal nature of blessing. It flows into us, through us, and out from us. Now we must model our hearts after Abraham, who "by faith. . .obeyed when he was called to go out to the place which he would receive as an inheritance," even though "he went out, not knowing where he was going" (Hebrews 11:8 NKJV). This is the totally surrendered faith that the Proverbs 31 woman had, and it is the faith we, too, are asked to have.

Doubt, though, is a normal part of human nature. When some spies were sent to scout out the Promised Land, they reported back that it would be hopeless to go there. Caleb and Joshua, however, were committed to a level of faith that allowed them to say with assurance: "If the LORD delights in us, he will bring us into this land and give it to us, a land that flows with milk and honey" (Numbers 14:8 ESV). We tend to put limits on what God can do. Even the things we think we really want, the best possible outcome we're imagining in our minds, however, limits what God longs to do for us. God wants to meet our needs beyond our wildest expectations. "Try Me now in this," God says in Malachi, and see if "I will not open for you the windows of heaven and pour out for you such blessing that there will not be room enough to receive it" (Malachi 3:10 NKJV).

This is not a selfish, me-first, Law-of-Attraction sort

of faith. Instead, it's the belief that the entire body of Christ will suffer if not all its members are healthy and nourished—and that includes ourselves. We will be blessed, and then we will be able to bless others. That's just the way this body works! As 1 Peter 3:9 says, "Bless—that's your job, to bless. You'll be a blessing and also get a blessing" (MSG).

We don't need to buy into a mind-set that looks at the world and sees only scarcity. If we spend time daily readjusting our thinking to align with the mind of Christ, until disbelief and discouragement drain out of us, we will be able to delight in being part of a healthy body where the blessings flow freely. God is waiting to "daily load us with benefits" (Psalm 68:19 NKJV).

Lord, make me a blessing to others today. You have given me so much. May Your abundant grace flow through me and out into the world.

The Wait

Sometimes we're so focused on the blessings we *don't* have yet that it's hard to be thankful for the blessings we already have. Like children, we hate to wait. We get impatient, and we forget that God sees from a perspective outside time. He knows that He plans to give us everything we need at exactly the right moment. While we wait on His timing, we need to cultivate a grateful heart for both the things we have—and the things for which we are still waiting.

In the Old Testament, the Lord commanded Israel to count their harvest, beginning the day after the Sabbath during Passover (Leviticus 23:15). For nearly two thousand years, the Jewish people had no homeland, and they had no harvest to count—and yet they continued to obey this Old Testament commandment. They counted a harvest that from the world's perspective simply didn't exist. We might feel foolish doing something like that, but they counted it as an act of faith, a visible demonstration of their faith in God.

In the New Testament, we're told that faith is the conviction of things not seen. This means we can begin to give thanks for blessings we have yet to receive. Like the Jewish people, we can count on a harvest that's yet to come. Whether it's guidance to know the right choice for our lives, healing for a wounded relationship or an ill loved one, or the answer to a painful problem, we can be grateful for the blessing that waits to be revealed. We don't know *how* God will bless us, but we know He *will*. All we have to do is be patient—and wait to see the unexpected blessings He will pour into our lives.

When we have in mind only one way that God can answer our prayers, though, we are limiting God. Our human perceptions pick out what seems so clearly to be the best possible solution to the situation—our friend's health needs to be healed, our husband needs to get a raise, our children need to have friends we like—that we may not notice what God is actually doing. With our minds fixed on our imaginary scenarios, we miss the abundance that's coming into being around us.

It's hard to believe in abundance when we're faced with the very real pain of death, the loss of a job, or fear for our children's well-being. And yet even in these situations, God is unfolding layers of bounty that we may not see until years—or a lifetime—later. It doesn't mean that His abundance isn't real. After all, the sun's shining just as brightly even when clouds hide it from our sight.

When clouds hide God's abundance from us, the best thing we can do is pray. "Don't worry about anything," Paul told the Philippians; "instead, pray about everything" (4:6 NLT).

Give me strength, Lord, to wait for Your timing.
Help me not to put limits on what You're doing in my life.
Teach me to let go of my own ideas
about what's best and simply trust.

A Commitment

If we want to be like the Proverbs 31 woman, we will make a commitment to opening our hearts to others (the emotional first step that will lead us to prayer) and then reaching out our hands (taking action). This commitment might look something like this:

Today I will first gratefully open my heart to all that God has given me. I will shift my attention away from my financial wealth so that I can see all the other riches God is giving me. I will appreciate my family and friends in new ways. I will notice the beauty of the natural world; I will appreciate the warmth of the sun, the green of leaves, the song of birds, the nourishment of rain. I will be open to receiving love from others, even if it comes to me in the smallest of ways (in the smile of a stranger, in the squeeze of my husband's hand, in a lopsided self-portrait from my child, in a compliment from a friend).

I promise next to bring the gift of myself to everyone I meet. Today, whatever I'm doing, wherever I am, I will give something to those I encounter, even if it's only a smile, a prayer, a small favor, or a compliment. I will open my heart to others so that God's love can flow out of me into the world. When I see specific opportunities where I can take action, I will do so, even if it's not convenient or seems impractical. I will not hoard my time, my money, my attention, or my talents. Instead, I will let them function as God intended them to, as part of the life-giving blood that flows through the body of Christ.

Mother Teresa, another strong woman who opened her heart and stretched out her hands, said, "Let us make one point, that we meet each other with a smile, when it is difficult to smile. Smile at each other, make time for each other." We may never know what something as small as a smile can mean to another soul. (I still remember a smile given to me on a day more than thirty years ago when my heart was sad and hurting; it came to me from a man I barely knew, and it opened in my heart a space where God's love could flow in and begin to heal me.) Steve Marboli, author of *Life, the Truth, and Being Free*, wrote, "Give yourself entirely to those around you. Be generous with your blessings. A kind gesture can reach a wound that only compassion can heal."

Fill me with compassion, I ask, Lord. May it be a healing stream that flows from Your heart to mine and out into the hearts of all those I encounter.

Focused Thinking

As we meditate on the meaning of Proverbs 31, here are quotes from other thinkers that may help us to focus our thinking while they strengthen our faith. Each one is like a present that grows and grows with us as we take time to unwrap it completely.

It's not how much we give but how much love we put into giving.
MOTHER TERESA

No one is useless in this world who lightens the burdens of another.
CHARLES DICKENS

We make a living by what we get. We make a life by what we give.
WINSTON CHURCHILL

Happiness doesn't result from what we get, but from what we give.
BEN CARSON

I must be willing to give whatever it takes to do good to others. This requires that I be willing to give until it hurts. Otherwise, there is no true love in me, and I bring injustice, not peace, to those around me.
MOTHER TERESA

I slept and I dreamed that life is all joy.
I woke and I saw that life is all service.
I served and I saw that service is joy.
KAHLIL GIBRAN

As we work to create light for others,
we naturally light our own way.
MARY ANNE RADMACHER

Give freely to the world these gifts of love and compassion.
Do not concern yourself with how much you receive in
return, just know in your heart it will be returned.
STEVE MARABOLI

Love only grows by sharing. You can only have more
for yourself by giving it away to others.
BRIAN TRACY

One must be poor to know the luxury of giving.
GEORGE ELIOT

No one has ever become poor by giving.
ANNE FRANK

Loving God, I thank You that so many others have gone
before me, learning the lessons of giving and receiving.
May I learn from their wisdom and make it my own.

PART XI

When it snows, she has no fear for her household;
for all of them are clothed in scarlet.
—VERSE 21 NIV

A Scarlet Thread

Hard times come to every family. Not every day is sunny and warm; some are cold and gloomy. But if we are like the Proverbs 31 woman, we do not need to fear. We will know they are clothed in scarlet!

Bible commentaries offer various interpretations of what the author meant when he talked about scarlet clothing. Scarlet dye was a luxury, used for the curtains of the Tabernacle (Exodus 26:1). It was the color of splendor, worn by the warriors of Israel (Nahum 2:3) and used for the cloth that covered the offerings in the Tabernacle (Numbers 4:8). It was the color of beauty, used to describe the lips of the beloved in the Song of Solomon (4:3). And it may also have foreshadowed the colors of salvation, for Christ was dressed in scarlet before the crucifixion (Matthew 27:28). Whatever its symbolism, it's clear that this woman's children are well provided for. They will not be shivering in the cold; instead, they'll be outside throwing snowballs in their bright red snowsuits!

But as mothers, our children's well-being may be the area of our lives where we worry most and trust least. Before I became a mother, the world seemed to me like a fairly safe and sunny place; but as soon as I held my first child in my arms, I was immediately flooded with fear. The world was suddenly full of dangers everywhere I turned. Germs, violence, and accidents threatened my beloved child, and I felt powerless to protect her, even though I intended to do my best.

And that is all we can do: our best. We can clothe our children with all our love—and then we have to leave them in God's hands. Meanwhile, we may still be afraid. There is so much unknown in our lives; it is only natural to feel frightened. Like an animal caught in the headlights of oncoming doom, we may feel like we're frozen, staring helplessly ahead, trying to see the path ahead before we dare to take a step, and all the while, life's dangers rush at our precious children.

But God can also use our love for our children to give us courage. The word *courage* comes from the Latin word for "heart"—and courage is born in the heart. Courageous acts come from the heart, and a courageous life is lived from the heart. Courage means we dress our children in the bright colors of hope, not in the dark shades of fear. And as we live our lives from our hearts, we discover the courage we need, entwined through our lives like a scarlet thread.

Lord, thank You for loving my children far more than even I do. Your love for them is limitless, and it will go with them places I can never go. Give me strength to send my children out into the world dressed in scarlet clothes, trusting them to Your eternal care.

Transformed Into Hope

Do you suppose the Proverbs 31 woman ever lay awake worrying about her children? I suspect she did, since most mothers do!

Not very many of us lie awake at night filled with hope. We're much more likely to lie there consumed with worries! Instead of imaging all the wonderful things God has in store for our children, we use our imaginations to picture scenarios of doom and dread. *What if such-and-such happens?* we think. And then we may find ourselves fleshing out exactly what that would look like, first one way and then another. *What if my son's best friend influences him to try drugs? What if my daughter catches the flu and ends up with pneumonia? What if my teenager gets in a car accident?* Dangers are everywhere, and they're not silly or far-fetched; they may be quite realistic. But that "such-and-such" we imagine is never something wonderful and happy. It's always something frightening or sad, something that fills our hearts with anxiety or downright terror.

As women, most of us seem prone to mulling things over in our minds. Even Mary, the mother of Jesus, "pondered" the events of Jesus' life in her heart (Luke 2:19). The pondering and mulling aren't necessarily bad things. New insights can come to us in the process. New awareness of God and others can also come from it. But that's only if we make the process a positive one instead of a negative one. Mulling over fears only makes them loom larger; pondering worries robs our hearts of optimism and hope.

The Bible tells us that prayer is the antidote to worry. When we turn our mulling into prayer, worry can be transformed into hope. But we need to practice using our imaginations in positive ways. Rick Warren wrote, "If you can worry, you can meditate, for worry is negative meditation." It's the focus of our thoughts that makes the difference between a positive meditation and a sleepless night of worry. When we turn our thoughts to God and His promises, our outlook changes. We begin to experience hope instead of worry. We can begin to rest in the knowledge that we've done our best to clothe our children to meet the world's dangers—and the rest is up to God (and to our children themselves). Adapting Psalm 37:5 to our own hearts, we can pray, "I commit my children to You, Lord. I trust them to Your care, knowing that You will do what I am trusting. I have done my best to clothe them in Your love—but You are the One who brings out from them the light of integrity and sound judgment. I take delight in what You will do for them, whatever it is."

Father God, when I catch myself worrying, remind me to give my fears to You. Stop the useless cycle of what-ifs and fix my mind on You.

A Protector And Guide

The Proverbs 31 woman faced the future without fear. She knew God's name and she was leaning on Him, knowing that He would not forsake her or her children (Psalm 9:10).

Our fears for our children come in many sizes, shapes, and forms. They may focus on their health or their school performance or their social skills. They may focus on the challenges of today, or they may anticipate what lies ahead. (*How will we pay for college? What if my child marries the wrong person? What if my child turns away from God?*) We interpret life's normal ups and downs as major catastrophes.

The great devotional author Oswald Chambers wrote:

> *The problems of life get hold of a man or woman and make it difficult to know whether in the face of these things he or she really is confident in Jesus Christ. The attitude of a believer must be "Things do look bad, but I believe Him; and when the whole thing is told I am confident my belief will be justified and God will be revealed as a God of love and justice." It does not mean that we won't have problems, but it does mean that our problems will never come in between us and our faith in Him. "Lord, I don't understand this, but I am certain*

*that there will be an explanation, and in the
meantime I put it to one side."* [11]

Author Phillip Keller had something similar
to say: "Too many of us are shaken up, frightened
and panicked by the storms of life. We claim to
have confidence in Christ but when the first dark
shadows sweep over us and the path we tread looks
gloomy we go into a deep slump of despair. . . .
This is not as it should be." When fear invades our
spirits, we need to turn to Jesus, who has promised
that He will never leave us, not today, not next year,
not ever (Matthew 28:20; Joshua 1:5). Keller went on
to say:

> *It is a most reassuring and reinforcing experience
> to the child of God to discover that there is,
> even in the dark valley, a source of strength and
> courage to be found in God. . . . Because He has
> led me through without fear before, He can do it
> again, and again, and again. In this knowledge
> fear fades and tranquility of heart and mind takes
> its place.* [12]

We may not understand today why certain
things happen in our children's lives; we may never
understand in this lifetime. But we can look back
and see how again and again God has worked out
the events of our lives. He will do the same for our

11. Oswald Chambers, *Daily Thoughts for Disciples* (Uhrichsville,
OH: Barbour, 2005).
12. Phillip Keller, *A Shepherd Looks at Psalm 23* (Grand Rapids:
Zondervan, 2008).

children. He will be their protector and guide. We can trust Him to command His angels to protect our children wherever they go. They will carry our children in their arms so they won't hurt their feet on life's stones (Psalm 91:11–12).

When dangers beset my children, Lord, remind me that You will never forsake them.

Choose Trust

As mothers, we need to be "fixing our eyes on Jesus, the pioneer and perfecter of faith. . .so that [we] will not grow weary and lose heart" (Hebrews 12:2-3 NIV). In the midst of our busy lives, however, when we so often find ourselves running on autopilot, it's easy to lose our spiritual eyes. We start seeing only the everyday external world, the mundane events of our lives. Our lives look like a series of tasks and duties strung together without meaning. We're getting through the days, but our eyes are no longer fixed on Jesus. As a result, we grow weary and we lose heart. Anxiety becomes the constant backdrop of our lives.

Trust is a choice, and it's one we need to make every day, each moment even. It is not an easy thing to do. It requires a greater consciousness of what is real. We need to turn off the autopilot and become truly present to our lives. We need to practice awareness of the here and now, this fleeting moment where God is waiting to meet us. When we do, we will discover the difference between merely functioning and *living*.

True living requires great discipline and focus. It takes a heart committed to living consciously and deliberately. It's the difference between climbing slowly and painfully down a cliff—and leaping out in the air in a hang glider! Letting go our grip on life seems risky—but it will lead to a new and exhilarating experience of what God can do in our lives and in the lives of our children.

"I am the door," Jesus said. "If anyone enters by

Me, he will be saved, and will go in and out and find pasture. . . . I have come that they may have life, and that they may have it more abundantly" (John 10:9–10 NKJV). Jesus also said, "I am the bread of life. Whoever comes to me will never go hungry" (John 6:35 NIV), and "I am the resurrection and the life. The one who believes in me will live, even though they die" (John 11:25 NIV).

Jesus is the doorway that enters into a richer, fuller, more exciting life. He is the bread that will nourish us with real life. And He can bring us back to life even when our hearts feel dead inside us. When He does, we will discover *true* life. It will be a life where we and our children can dance joyfully, all of us clothed in the scarlet garments of God's splendor.

Dearest Lord, help me not to be content with plodding through my days, merely functioning. I want to enter through the doorway of Your heart into something better. I choose to truly live.

Surrender

When a child is sick, all parents suffer. The Gospel of Mark tells about a father who brought his demon-possessed son to Jesus and said, "If you can do anything, take pity on us and help us" (Mark 9:22 NIV). Jesus seemed surprised that there should be any question in the father's mind that He could do something, and then Jesus said, "Everything is possible for one who believes" (Mark 9:23 NIV). The father gave an answer that many of us would have to say as well: "I do believe; help me overcome my unbelief!" (Mark 9:24 NIV).

The human mind is like that. One moment it's resting peacefully and confidently in its belief in God—and the next moment, it's jumped up with a whole list of "buts" and "what-ifs." Those are the kinds of thoughts that keep us awake at night. We may finally get our minds quieted enough that we can fall asleep, only to wake up in the morning to a fresh batch of doubt.

We need to remind ourselves that our *feelings* of anxiety don't reflect true reality, and neither do our anxious, doubtful thoughts. We don't need to feel guilty about our doubt and worry. We don't need to try to squash them down into a shape that looks more spiritual, more Christian. Instead, we can identify what we're experiencing, accept it, and then let it go, knowing that it's just something that will naturally come and go. It doesn't tell us anything about what's really real, and it becomes just one more piece of our hearts that we surrender to God.

Even the disciples had trouble surrendering their fear to God. They lived daily with Jesus, they saw the amazing things He could do, and yet they still got scared. When they saw Jesus walking on the water toward them, they even thought He was a ghost. They were terrified. The Gospel of Matthew says that Jesus called to them, "Take courage. It is I. Don't be scared!"

When Peter heard that, he called across the water, "If it's really You, Jesus, tell me to come to You across the water."

"Go ahead," Jesus answered.

Peter got out of the boat and did the impossible: he walked on water. But then he did what we all do; he started to notice "reality." He lost his focus on Jesus, and he began to pay more attention to the messages his human senses brought to him about what was going on around him in the external world. The wind was whipping his robe; the waves were heaving under his feet. He must have thought to himself, *What in the world am I doing?*

When Peter shifted his attention away from Jesus, he was immediately swamped with anxiety. He sank into the water—and into his fear. But Jesus didn't stand by and let him drown. The Lord immediately reached out and caught Peter. "Oh Peter," he said, "you man of such little faith! Why did you doubt Me?" (See Matthew 14:22–31.)

Author Matthew Henry wrote, "The strongest faith and the greatest courage have a mixture of fear. Those that can say, *Lord, I believe*; must say, *Lord, help my unbelief.*" As parents, we, too, can be honest with the Lord about our fears. When they threaten to drown us, we can ask for His help. He is our loving and patient Friend, and He will never punish us for our doubt.

Father God, right now I give You my fear and worries for my children. Remind me to give them to You all over again as many times as I need reminding.

Faithful God

Fear is a part of our human nature. It can even be healthy. Our fear response is a part of our makeup that's designed to protect us from physical dangers. Psychologists and scientists talk about our fight-or-flight response, which is the reaction that fear has on our bodies. Fear makes our hearts beat faster and our lungs work harder. It dilates our pupils so we can see better and sends extra blood to our muscles. All those physical responses get us ready to either fight a danger or run away from it. Our fear response can save our lives.

According to psychologists, anxiety and worry are different from fear. Fear is what we feel when we're confronted with an actual danger that's right there in front of us, demanding that we take immediate action. It's what we feel when the angry dog bursts out at us from our neighbor's yard, when the car swerves in front of us on the highway, or when our kitchen bursts into flames. Anxiety, however, say psychologists, is what we feel when we encounter a danger that's less definite. If our child has a serious illness, for example, the presence of danger is very real, but we feel helpless to deal with it. Our bodies' responses don't help us. We can't run away from this danger, and we can't slug it with our fists. This sort of helpless fear makes us feel physically sick.

Anxiety is also what we feel when we face imaginary dangers. Lying awake in the dark, the "what-ifs" loom like monsters over our children. If we could, we'd go to battle for our children; we'd swoop them up in our arms and run with them to safety. But what can we do to fight something that's imaginary? How can we escape its reach? Since it lives only inside our own minds, it goes with us wherever we go. Once again, our bodies' normal, healthy fear responses have no outlet. They turn into stress that can make us physically ill and rob the joy from our lives.

God does not condemn us for feeling anxiety. The Bible says, "As a father has compassion on his children, so the Lord has compassion on those who fear him" (Psalm 103:13 niv). But God doesn't want us to suffer unnecessary fear when we really don't need to. He longs to bring peace to our tormented minds and rest to our exhausted bodies. Jesus said that the peace He gives us is not like the world's peace (John 14:27); in other words, it's not based on external events. It's a peace that continues on undisturbed by both fear and anxiety.

Trusting God to protect our children grows a little easier with practice. As we see the faithful ways God has cared for them in the past, we can begin to expect Him to offer them the same care today and in the future. But on the days when our fears seem too great to bear, God understands. All He asks is that we give Him our anxiety and doubt, just as we give Him our joy and love. He treasures the gift of our negative emotions as much as He does the gift of our more positive emotions.

Today, God, no matter how hard I try, I can't seem to overcome my anxieties. I'm going to stop trying to fight them; I'm going to just give them to You. Transform them, I pray, into something new and lovely.

171

PART XII

She makes coverings for her bed;
she is clothed in fine linen and purple.
—VERSE 22 NIV

A Lovely Place Of Rest

After all those things that the Proverbs 31 woman does that have to do with caring for others, now we see that she hasn't been neglecting herself meanwhile. She makes her bed—her private place—lovely and comfortable. She dresses in clothing that becomes her and is suited to her true dignity and identity. She knows that she needs and deserves her own attention and care.

What would it mean if we followed her example? Well, it might mean something quite literal: we straighten up our bedrooms and buy new bedspreads, creating lovely places of rest where we can withdraw and find relaxation and rest; we assess our wardrobes with the same loving attention we give our children's school clothes. We might also, however, look further and find the symbolism in this verse.

As modern women, we're often not as wise as the Proverbs 31 woman. Many of us have learned to always put ourselves last. Especially if we're mothers, that seems to come with the territory. We may resent doing this, but we still believe it's what all good mothers have to do. We even assume that God must approve of our unselfish behavior. We may feel a little glow of self-righteous martyrdom.

But the truth is, God doesn't put a mother's needs last. When He looks at our families, He sees that everyone deserves time and attention; He doesn't ask one specific individual to do all the family's dirty work. Instead, He loves and treasures each of us, including those of us who are mothers.

He wants to bless us all. He wants the whole family to be nourished and cared for, and He would never want mothers to be emotionally and spiritually—and sometimes physically—undernourished. Because He understands our inner selves, He knows we can't keep taking care of our families indefinitely if we never take care of ourselves. He wants to nourish us all—and He wants to help us mothers take better care of ourselves.

Take a minute to look at your life. Pretend that it's not your own life but the life of a beloved friend or a grown child. If you're honest, what would you advise the person living this life to change? Here are some questions to consider:

- Is this person eating in a healthy way?
- Does this person get the exercise she needs?
- Is she getting enough sleep?
- Are her needs being respected by those around her?
- Does she have opportunities to express her creativity?
- Does she have enough laughter and joy in her life?
- Is she doing too much? Has she bitten off more than she can chew in one or more areas of her life?
- How is she hurting herself by ignoring her own needs?
- What effect does her self-neglect have on the rest of the family?

Show me, patient Lord, where I am not being true to my own self. Remind me that You live within me—and that as I respect and care for my own body, mind, and heart, I am also caring for You.

In God's Eyes

All of us need to have the healthy sense of our own worth that the Proverbs 31 woman had. To have that doesn't mean we're conceited; humility and self-worth are very comfortable partners.

But too often we try to derive our self-worth from sources that sooner or later let us down. If we count on our jobs or our relationships or our appearance to make us feel good about ourselves, we're bound to run into disappointment. So long as we are experiencing success—we get a promotion at work, we make a new friend, we lose ten pounds—we feel proud and full of self-esteem. But eventually, inevitably, we find that in one way or another we have failed. We lose the job we love, a friend betrays us, we regain the weight we lost. When these things happen, if we have pinned huge chunks of our self-worth to them, a terrible blow is struck to our identities. Anyone would feel hurt and sadness when confronted with situations like these, but too often we act as though these external factors are telling an objective truth about us. We have lost sight of the true meaning of who we are.

Take appearance as a good example of what we're talking about. We live in a world where all too often we judge each other by how closely our outward appearances conform to the current fashion. We act as though there were some absolute standard for clothing, hair, and weight—but all you have to do is walk through an art museum, and the paintings from various eras will reveal that the human concept of what's beautiful in terms of clothes, hairstyle, and body shape has changed drastically from century to century. We twenty-first-century women often feel embarrassed if we have plump, pear-shaped bodies; yet those very same bodies in an earlier era would have matched the epitome of feminine loveliness. Back then, women with thin, willowy bodies would have been beating themselves up instead!

We need to find our self-worth somewhere other than the world's changeable whims and our external appearances. We are eternal beings, inhabitants of God's everlasting kingdom. Our bodies and our performance in various areas of our lives are only two aspects of who we are. They are a precious part of our identities, and they deserve our care—but who we really are, who we are in God's eyes, goes far beyond the world's fickle judgments.

Jesus, teach me to look to You as the source of my self-worth. Remind me not to depend on the exterior world to tell me what I'm worth. I want to see with Your eyes.

Support Networks

Often as mothers we are tempted to set aside our own health needs and concerns because we are too busy focusing on what must be done for our families. During pregnancy, however, we were probably more careful of our bodies than at any other time in our lives. We recognized that our habits, our sleep patterns, and our diets would all directly affect the life growing inside us. We realized we could not separate our own life from the child's. Baby and mother were intimately connected, blood flowing between their bodies.

Once our babies are born, though, we often forget ourselves as we focus on these demanding new creatures. During the first days and weeks (and sometimes months) after birth, it's difficult to find time for the sleep we need, let alone time to worry about our bed coverings! We can barely take a shower, so we're certainly not dressing up in purple and linen. Unless we have lots of help from family and friends, it's hard to avoid that desperate postpartum exhaustion that spills into the hormonal depression we're already feeling. Luckily, those weary days don't last forever.

If they do—if our children are no longer infants and we're still exhausted and depressed—we need to get help. We will probably need to ask for it instead of silently hoping that someone will notice how desperate we are and offer to help us.

The first step is probably to be honest with our

husbands and let them know we need help. That doesn't mean we scream all our desperation and rage at them and expect them to respond positively. It doesn't even mean that our husbands have to be the ones to fix the situation; objectively their lives may already be filled with heavy responsibilities and tight schedules. We do, however, need our husbands' support and understanding. We need them to encourage us and help us find the help we need.

We should also reach out to our support networks. Friends, family members, pastors, and members of our congregation may be able to offer practical help. We need to talk to our doctors and get their professional advice. They may be able to spot ways we could adjust our lives to create a healthier balance for us. They may want to run tests to determine if a physical problem is partly or totally the cause of our difficulties. We may need medication. Counseling might help.

We may be embarrassed to admit that we're not coping with our lives, but this is something we need to do not only for ourselves but also for our children. We're no longer pregnant, but our health and well-being still have direct effects on our children's. The metaphor that's often used to illustrate this is the directions flight attendants give parents at the beginning of every flight: "In the event of an accident, oxygen masks will drop from overhead. Don't try to assist your child until you have secured your own mask." The parent's first instinct may be to put the child's safety first, just as our instinct is to put our children's daily needs ahead of our own, but following this instinct in these situations might actually put the child in danger. We won't be able to help our children put on their oxygen masks if we're unconscious. And we're not much more use to our children when we're so exhausted that our emotions are frazzled and our patience is in pieces.

The Proverbs 31 woman knew this. She took care of herself. If she hadn't, she would never have been able to accomplish all the other things she did.

I ask You, Jesus, to show me if I need help coping with my life. I trust that You will bring the helpers I need into my life.

Renewed Energy

A woman's physical exhaustion is a very real problem. If we get the help we need, though, we usually know that with time to relax and sleep, we'll feel better. But emotional and spiritual exhaustion go hand in hand with physical, and it may be more difficult to find ways to refresh our minds, hearts, and souls.

Here are some practical ideas to consider implementing in our lives. We might consider them the twenty-first-century versions of fine bed coverings and linen clothing!

- Keep a journal. Make it a place to acknowledge and affirm your own accomplishments and successes, even the tiniest ones.
- Let go of your need for perfection. No one's going to give you a bad grade if you go to bed with a dirty house! The fashion police aren't going to arrest your child for wearing the same shirt she did earlier this week.
- Acknowledge your own feelings. Don't try to push them away. Make room for them in your heart, as though they are children who need to be loved. Picture Jesus seated at the center of your heart, with that crowd of needy children gathered around Him. Listen to what they tell Him. Be willing to learn from them.
- Listen to your body. This will take some practice, because we've grown so accustomed to smothering our bodies' voices. If you let

it, however, your body will tell you when something is wrong. Does your headache mean you need to simplify your life? Does your tiredness tell you that you need to go to bed earlier? Are you hungry—or not? When we listen to our bodies' actual hunger messages (instead of eating for emotional reasons), we may naturally go back to a healthier weight.

☞ Practice saying no when you're asked to do something. You may literally need to stand in front of a mirror and practice saying the word! The more you say it, the easier it will come to your lips. The world will not end if you disappoint someone!

☞ Create sanctuaries and sabbaths in your life—places and times where you can withdraw from all the demands on your life and be replenished. If you have young children who need supervision, you may need to ask for help with this one from your husband, a family member, or a friend. It may even be worth spending the money on a babysitter so that you can escape at least once a week.

Lord, when I'm spiritually, mentally, and emotionally exhausted, show me the actions I need to take to care for myself. You know that when I'm so terribly weary, it's hard to find the energy to make a change, even a change that will help me feel better. Give me the energy I need, I pray, to care for myself.

Caring For You!

Here are a few more ways we might consider caring for ourselves. Adding even one or two of these to our lives is a step toward showing ourselves the respect and love we deserve.

- ↝ Practice good hygiene and take care of your appearance. Even if you're going to be home all day by yourself doing housework, taking the time to look good will help you feel better about yourself. This does not mean thinking that we have more value when we look good. It's just the opposite. Because we have value, we deserve the care necessary to look our best.

- ↝ Make time for friends. If you're too busy to spend time with people who understand you, you'll end up feeling lonely and isolated. Friends can help you have a better sense of perspective on problems. They may be able to see solutions more clearly than you can. They can give you emotional support. But be certain that the people you choose to spend time with are true friends. Do you feel encouraged after you've been with them—or do you feel even more depressed than before you got together? As the Bible says, you need friends who will "edify" you. The word comes from a Latin root that meant "to construct, to build something." Hang out with people who build you up, and avoid the ones who tear you down.

- Try to do something you enjoy every day. That might mean dancing, reading a good book, watching a favorite TV show, working in the garden, painting, or doing something else that's creative.
- Find ways to relax, and include them in your life weekly, if not daily. It might be taking a candlelit bath. It might be going for a walk in the woods or getting a massage. It might be having sex with your husband!
- Listen to music throughout the day, whenever it's practical. Music has the power to lift our emotions and give us a greater sense of energy.
- Set aside time when you limit your connections with the world. Don't let outside voices invade your home and thoughts every minute of the day.

Loving God, I ask that You show me practical routines I can build into my life that will help me take better care of myself. Remind me that I'm worth it!

Unplug

Our Proverbs 31 woman's life was busy and full of big responsibilities, but there are some challenges she never had to face. One of those is the constant connection we have today with others through cell phones, e-mail, and Facebook. We've all grown so accustomed to these connections that they feel normal and necessary. But we all need to unplug sometimes.

For example, I find myself checking my e-mail often throughout my workdays. It feels a little like picking up the "Chance" card in Monopoly: What will have come in this time? It could be a message from a friend asking for a lunch date. It might be a business opportunity. It's often a professional problem that needs my attention. I've realized, however, that when I do this, I'm giving away my power to control my own time. I'm always reacting instead of being proactive. At the end of the workday, I often feel as though I didn't get as much done as I'd hoped. I blame my lack of productivity on all those constant interruptions from my e-mail—and yet I sought them out. It's my own fault that I gave my e-mail priority.

Communicating with others is a necessary part of our lives. It's a way to exchange ideas, information, and love. But sometimes we all need moments of silence and solitude. In the Gospels, we're told that Jesus took time to withdraw from the crowds to a secluded place where He could be all alone. He didn't take even His closest friends with Him. He knew that any interruptions would shatter the quiet time He needed to get in touch with His Father.

Now imagine if Jesus had had a cell phone with Him. He put it on vibrate and dropped it in His pocket, then knelt on the ground and bowed His head. The wind whispered through the trees, He heard a birdcall, and He and the Father were one. . .and then, "Bzzzzz!" A text message had just come in, but He decided to ignore it. His phone was set to keep signaling Him until He looked at the message, though, so finally, He had to pull out His phone, intending to just open and close it so it would stop buzzing. He couldn't help glancing at the message, though.

It was from Peter. "Master," it said, "we need to ask You something. Could You give us a call?" Jesus sighed. It probably wasn't anything important, but maybe it was. And He loved His disciples and wanted to help them in any way He could. "It probably won't take long," He told Himself as He dialed Peter's number.

Forty-five minutes later, Jesus finally closed His phone and settled Himself again on the ground. "Where were We, Father?" He tuned in to the quiet noises of this secluded place. . .and then, "Bzzzzz!"

This is a silly story, of course. If cell phones had been invented during Bible times, Jesus would never have brought one with Him when He went to a lonely place to pray. He was wise enough to know that He needed time away from the crowds and all the demands on His life—and He would have been disciplined enough to completely unplug from the outer world so that He could plug into the world of His Father.

The Proverbs 31 woman made her bed beautiful. It was a place where she could relax and be refreshed.

We also get the sense that she carried within her, throughout her busy days, the sense of peace and serenity she found in her alone times. If we, too, hope to create both inner and outer places of private quiet, we must have the wisdom and discipline to sometimes turn off our e-mail and cell phones.

God, I need to receive Your messages more than I need to read any e-mail or text message. Remind me that I need to unplug from the world sometimes if I want to hear Your still, small voice.

PART XIII

Her husband is respected at the city gate,
where he takes his seat among the elders of the land.
—VERSE 23 NIV

Steadiness

The Proverbs 31 woman is an asset to her husband. She supports and strengthens his reputation. Clearly, however, she is not the "little woman behind the great man," since she engages in her own work and makes independent decisions. Remember that the author of Proverbs also may have been drawing parallels between his ideal woman and Lady Wisdom as she is described in the book of Ecclesiastes. The sort of woman the author had in mind may have helped her husband with her wisdom—her accurate insights and thoughtful judgments. Her steadiness gave him balance. She protected his reputation and was loyal to him; she stood by her man! Do we have that same commitment to our husbands? Can our husbands count on our steady love, wisdom, and support?

We may feel that we don't have it in us to give our husbands the wise support that the Proverbs 31 woman gave hers. Married love doesn't always come easily. It's hard work learning the compromises and strategies that will make our marriages work.

We often think of stubbornness as a negative quality. When it comes to marriage, though, our love needs to be stubborn so that it doesn't give up easily. We need to love tenaciously. At its roots, *tenacity* means "the act of holding fast, of being steadfast, firm." This is the way we need to love our husbands: steadfastly, holding tight to our commitment despite the ups and downs of married life.

All married partners let each other down at one

time or another. But even when we cannot find the way to married harmony, we can continue to pray for our husbands. Our prayer support can be steady and constant. We can ask that God supply our husbands with wisdom when our own fails.

The apostle Paul showed this same kind of committed love when he wrote to the church at Ephesus. "I. . .do not cease to give thanks for you," he wrote, "making mention of you in my prayers: that the God of our Lord Jesus Christ, the Father of glory, may give to you the spirit of wisdom and revelation in the knowledge of Him" (Ephesians 1:15–17 NKJV). We can pray in the same way for our husbands.

If we follow Paul's example of prayer, we will daily, constantly express our gratitude for our husbands; thankfulness will weave through our prayers for our husbands. We will pray stubbornly, tenaciously, refusing to give up (even when we are angry or hurt). We will ask God to give our husbands "a spirit of wisdom." We will pray that God will reveal Himself to them.

Help me, Lord, to be a steady support to my husband. Use me to bless him. Remind me to pray for him often with gratitude. I ask that Your light shine on him today.

Affirmation

"Let us stop just *saying* we love people," wrote John in his first epistle. "Let us *really* love them, and *show it* by our *actions*" (1 John 3:18 TLB). *I love you* are important words in any marriage, but sometimes we need to stop and check to see if our actions match up with our words. It's easy to automatically say, "I love you," but not so easy to be patient, to bite back words that might hurt, or to hold on to our tempers when our husbands are driving us crazy!

C. S. Lewis wrote, "The most precious gift that marriage gave me was this constant impact of something very close and intimate yet all the time unmistakably other, resistant—in a word, real." As silly as it sounds, sometimes we forget that our husbands are real. We take them for granted. We go to sleep next to them, wake up beside them, shuffle responsibilities with them for kids and cars and meals, but we may never stop to wonder what is going on inside their heads. If they're unhappy, do we notice? Are we glad when they're happy? Do we take pride in their accomplishments? Do we laugh with them? Do we listen when they talk (*really* listen)?

If commitment is the foundation on which marriage is built, then communication is what forms marriage's structure. Communication involves both giving and receiving. It requires a back-and-forth exchange of ideas and feelings with our husbands. It also requires respect. If you're screaming at your husband or insulting him, it's not likely that real communication is taking place.

Communication doesn't always need to be verbal. Some people are more comfortable with talking than others. If we have silent husbands, as some of us do, we can ask that they make an effort to talk a little more—but we also need to respect their reticence. When we pay attention, we may notice the ways these wordless men communicate their love and respect to us. They may be thoughtful in little ways. They may be tender in bed, intent on our pleasure. Maybe there are things we've come to take for granted—the way our husbands warm up the car for us in the morning, for example, or the fact that they never fail to buy our favorite ice cream for us—and when we think about it, we may realize that all these are "I love yous" sprinkled through our daily lives.

Affirmation should be a frequent element of our communication with our husbands. We need to let them know that we notice the things they do for us. We need to compliment them when they look good (even if they pretend not to care). We need to show our pride in their achievements and mention to them the strengths we see in them. When we communicate affirmation to our husbands, we are supporting them the way the Proverbs 31 woman clearly supported her husband. We are building them up, not tearing them down with anger and insults.

Of course we want our husbands to do the same thing for us. We want to feel affirmed, too! But as Francis of Assisi prayed, we need to seek to understand more than we worry about being understood. If we hold back our affirmation from our husbands because we're hurt and resentful, we create an atmosphere where hurt feelings and resentment get passed back and forth. When we work instead to build a structure filled with love and security, our husbands may find that within its shelter they can more easily express their love and affirmation.

Lord, bless my marriage. Remind me to notice my husband, to pay attention to his reality. Help us to communicate with each other more. May I show him my affirmation in little ways today.

Love Defined

In his first letter to the Corinthians, the apostle Paul spelled out a practical definition of love. His definition had fourteen elements, which we can apply to our marriages.

1. *Love is patient.* It picks up the dirty socks a spouse always leaves in the middle of the floor; it holds its tongue instead of snapping in anger.

2. *Love is kind.* It doesn't insult a husband; it is gentle with his weaknesses; it goes out of its way to do something nice for a husband.

3. *Love does not envy.* It doesn't begrudge a husband's good fortune (for example, his promotion at work when we failed to get the one we'd hoped for in our own career); it doesn't long to possess (or throw away!) a husband's belongings; it rejoices over the things that make a husband happy.

4. *Love does not boast.* It doesn't try to impress a husband by bragging about its own accomplishments; it doesn't try to inflate its own worth by exaggerating achievements.

5. *Love is not proud.* It is never arrogant; instead, it is always humble, always willing to be respectful of a husband.

6. *Love is not rude.* It isn't inconsiderate of a husband's feelings; it pays attention to his wishes.

7. *Love is not self-seeking.* It doesn't put self ahead of a husband but instead sets self to one side.

8. *Love is not easily angered.* It isn't touchy or irritable; it doesn't have a short fuse.

9. *Love keeps no record of wrongs.* It doesn't harp over and over back to something that happened long ago; it doesn't bring up the same list of grievances every time there's a conflict.

10. *Love does not delight in evil but rejoices in the truth.* It's never glad when a husband runs into trouble; it does not gloat or gossip (even with its closest girlfriends).

11. *Love always trusts, and it believes all things.* It gives a husband the benefit of the doubt; it is loyal; it gives him a second (and third and fourth) chance.

12. *Love always hopes.* It always looks toward the future; it believes that a husband is capable of living out his fullest potential.

13. *Love always perseveres.* It doesn't give up on a husband; it endures through the hard times.

14. *Love goes on forever.* It is eternal, unending, unlimited, and unconditional.

This is the same sort of love that Christ gives to us. If we want our marriages to grow and flourish, we will follow His pattern for love. We will look for opportunities to lay down our lives, to put our love into practice. In the context of our marriages, this seldom means we literally give up our lives for the men we love. More likely, it means we pick up their dry cleaning—or take out the trash for them when they're running late!

Teach me, Lord God, to love my husband as You love me.

PART XIV

She makes linen garments and sells them,
and supplies the merchants with sashes.
—VERSE 24 NIV

Expanded Creativity

Once again our ideal woman is engaged in a business enterprise. That woman! She's a little like the Energizer Bunny: she just never quits. Instead of feeling intimidated by this woman's terrifying level of strength and initiative (which I confess to feeling!), we need to seek what we can learn from this new aspect of the woman's personality.

Perhaps what we see here is her willingness to try new things. All of us tend to fall in ruts. Ruts are familiar. They're comfortable. Even if they're boring, they feel safe. They don't ask us to change. Don't require that we try something new—something that we may not be good at.

But sometimes God asks us to step out of our ruts. He asks us to expand our creativity—and also, like the Proverbs 31 woman, reap its reward. When we do, we will find that trying something new has many benefits besides just breaking the boredom!

When we try something new, even if we're not completely successful at it, we gain new confidence in ourselves. As a kid, I struck out every time we played softball during gym class. Understandably, no one wanted me on their team. I dreaded being up to bat, and each time, I was filled with such embarrassment that I could barely stand, let alone hit a ball with a bat. As an adult, if friends were playing a softball game for fun, I found a reason to leave the gathering. I intended to never again face the sense of failure and embarrassment I'd experienced as a kid. Then one day, my husband persuaded me to give softball one more try. He told me how to stand, he told me how to hold the bat, he told me how to swing—and to my amazement, I smacked the ball into the outfield on my first try. I haven't turned into a hotshot softball player; I'll never consider it to be one of my skills. But just the fact that I'd had the courage to do it as an adult gave me the heady feeling that I could do pretty much *anything*.

Going out on a limb to try something new takes courage. Proving to yourself that you can do it gives you a new confidence that can spill over into other areas of your life.

Trying something new may also give us opportunities to learn new things and gain new ideas. Our lives will be enriched—and we will pass the wealth on to our families and communities.

Lord, show me if there is something new I should try— and give me the courage to step up to bat and take that swing!

Comfort Zone

From the time we were babies, we've based our understanding of how the world works on the experiences we've already had. The sun rose in the morning for the past seven days (as well as the past several thousands of years), so we assume that it will also rise tomorrow. The sun rising is a part of our reality, and in this case, our perception of reality is accurate. When we base our understanding of who we are, however, on ways that we've behaved in the past, we limit ourselves. We think to ourselves, *I've always been that way, so how could I possibly change?*—and we really believe it. It just doesn't seem very likely that we'll change in any major way.

What we may not realize is that it's not so much that we're incapable of change as that the thought of changing scares us. Another name for a rut is a comfort zone!

We all have comfort zones. They're made up of familiar routines, actions, and places. They're predictable, and we find that reassuring and comforting. Comfort zones give us *comfort*, and that's not a bad thing, especially in times of stress and pain.

But the Proverbs 31 woman wasn't afraid to leave her comfort zone and try her hand at something new. She didn't set limits on her ability to grow and learn. She was willing to break free from the past, from the familiar and safe, and take the risk of a new enterprise.

Not all of us have her courage. Our woman's past had already taught her that she was completely capable of learning something new. (After all, she had already learned to manage a household, buy a field, plant a vineyard, and spin thread!) To match her level of self-confidence, we may need to practice leaving our comfort zones in small ways. Each time we do, we will find we have new courage to take on the next challenge.

Sherman Finesilver, an American federal judge, had this to say about trying new things:

> *Keep these concepts in mind: You've failed many times, although you don't remember. You fell down the first time you tried to walk. You almost drowned the first time you tried to swim. . . . Don't worry about failure. My suggestion to each of you: Worry about the chances you miss when you don't even try.*[13]

In the book of Revelation, God says, "Look, I am making everything new!" (21:5 NLT). Can we dare to let Him make us new, too?

God, thank You that the world is full of new things to try. Thank You for waiting to reveal Yourself in new ways, as I have the courage to step out of my comfort zones.

---

13. David DeFord, *1000 Brilliant Achievement Quotes: Advice from the World's Wisest*. (Omaha: Ordinary People Can Win! 2004).

Something New!

If you want to build your self-confidence and your ability to try something new, here are some suggestions you might consider for giving you practice:

- Take a cooking, art, or fitness class.
- Take music lessons, join a community theatre company, or join a church or community choir.
- Try a type of food you always assumed you didn't like. (In my case, that would be beets! I recently realized that I really had no idea how beets taste; I had just assumed throughout my entire life that I didn't like them.)
- Visit a new church. (That doesn't mean you have to leave your old church, just because it's familiar. But you may find that you learn new things from other churches' styles of worship, liturgy, or ideas.)
- Volunteer for an organization in your community.
- Talk to someone at work or church whom you've never talked to before.
- Make a date to spend some time with one of the people you've dared to talk to and get to know her better.

These all may seem like small, trivial things—but just reading some of them may fill us with resistance. We can fight that resistance with these strategies:

- Stop thinking of yourself as weak or incompetent. Focus on your strengths.
- Practice eliminating the words *wish*, *hope*, *maybe*, and *should* from your daily conversation and thoughts. Replace them with *can*, *will*, and *do*.
- Take small steps—and be proud of them. Even the longest journeys are made up of small, individual steps.
- Stop procrastinating—and justifying it to others and yourself with excuses.
- Ask your friends and family to support and encourage you in the new thing you're trying.
- Take a friend along with you. New things are often not so intimidating when we do them with someone familiar at our side.

You may not succeed at whatever it is that you try—but just the fact that you attempted it will still help you to grow. You will discover that you do have the strength to try new things—and that you can survive failure. You may even discover that you can learn things from your failures that are useful in the next new thing you try!

God, I ask that You step out with me into a new adventure. Thank You that You will always be at my side. No matter what I try, You will never abandon me.

Be Courageous

The fear of trying something new is a part of most human beings. And yet countless people have overcome their fears. If they hadn't, we would all be living exactly the way Adam and Eve lived!

Here are quotes from people who dared to venture out into the unfamiliar. We can be encouraged by their courage. Their wisdom, forged in the midst of unfamiliar ventures, can give us confidence to also dare new things.

Do one thing every day that scares you.
—ELEANOR ROOSEVELT

Do not be too timid and squeamish about your actions. All life is an experiment.
—RALPH WALDO EMERSON

*I am always doing things I can't do—
that's how I learn to do them.*
—PABLO PICASSO

Everyone has a "risk muscle." You keep it in shape by trying new things. If you don't, it atrophies. Make a point of using it at least once a day.
—ROGER VON OECH

The greatest failure is the failure to try.
—WILLIAM WARD

To dare is to lose one's footing momentarily.
To not dare is to lose oneself.
—SØREN KIERKEGAARD

Progress always involves risks. You can't steal
second base and keep your foot on first.
—FREDERICK B. WILCOX

You'll always miss 100 percent of the shots you don't take.
—WAYNE GRETZKY

A ship in harbor is safe—but that is not what ships are for.
—JOHN A. SHEDD

Why not go out on a limb? Isn't that where the fruit is?
—FRANK SCULLY

Yes, risk taking is inherently failure-prone. Otherwise,
it would be called sure-thing-taking.
—TIM MCMAHON

Jesus, Friend of my soul, thank You for all the
brave humans who have dared to take a risk.
Thank You that You were willing to risk
everything, even Your life, for my salvation.

PART XV

She is clothed with strength and dignity;
she can laugh at the days to come.
—VERSE 25 NIV

A Powerful Woman

In Hebrew, this description of our wonder-woman has this literal meaning: "Power and splendor are her clothes. The future makes her smile; it makes her playful with amusement."

If we had any illusions left that the Proverbs 31 woman would fit comfortably in the traditional image of a "good Christian woman," this verse would finally dispel them. This woman is no weak, submissive, soft-spoken lady. She is *powerful*. Splendor and strength are her everyday clothes.

Does this mean that in some ways she's masculine? After all, we're accustomed to thinking of strength as a masculine quality. We often think of strength as aggressive and forceful, but the Proverbs 31 woman has her own brand of strength. It lies in her capacity to apply wisdom and insight to each situation she encounters. It is expressed by her compassion, as well as her creativity and ingenuity. She does not need to imitate a man to be effective at what she does. Instead, she puts her own unique abilities to good use. Her compassion and wisdom demonstrate her power.

Despite the changes that the women's rights movement has brought to our world, we often overlook this kind of strength. As women, even as we compete with men in the workplace, we may find ourselves imitating masculine traits, rather than tapping into our own strengths. We may even feel that our emotions put us at a disadvantage in the professional world.

If we model ourselves after the Proverbs 31 woman, though, we will begin to recognize our own strengths of insight and compassion. We will learn to put them to use, both at home and in our workplaces. We will use them to give new energy to our relationships. They will aid our decision-making and empower our work.

Blogger Renee Wade has this to say about a woman's strength: "A strong woman is one who feels deeply and loves fiercely. Her tears flow just as abundantly as her laughter. A strong woman is both soft and powerful. She is both practical and spiritual. A strong woman in her essence is a gift to all the world."

As women, we sometimes feel we lack strength and courage to face the world's dangers. That feeling isn't an accurate perception of our own reality, however. We don't need to be shy or timid, for God has made us strong. He has clothed us with splendor and dignity.

Are we strong enough to share the gift of ourselves with the world?

Dearest Lord, thank You for giving me strength and splendor. Help me to recognize those qualities in myself—and then use them to Your glory.

The Unknown

The second half of verse 25 speaks to our attitude about the future. How many of us look into the unknown days that lie ahead and smile? Do we anticipate them with the playful anticipation a child feels before Christmas morning? Or are we filled with dread when we think about the future?

From one perspective, fearing the future makes sense. If what we fear most is death—both ours and our loved ones'—then that which we fear does indeed wait for us further down the road. We will all grow old. Our bodies will lose their strength. One day, sooner or later, we will die. To try to think anything else would be to refuse to accept reality. But that is exactly what our culture does. It pretends that we can be young forever (if we use the right face cream). It hides death out of sight where we can do our best not to see its face.

And yet everyone who is born must one day die. As we hold our newborn babies in our arms, their deaths await them in the future, no matter how much it pains us to think that. Death is an unavoidable part of life.

When the Proverbs 31 woman smiled at the future, she wasn't pretending that she didn't know that the day of her death would one day arrive. Instead, I think she faced that fact head-on—and laughed with joy. She made a joke, not to dismiss the reality of death but to lay claim on its *true* reality.

This is what Paul was talking about in his first

epistle to the Corinthians when he wrote, "O death, where is thy sting? O grave, where is thy victory?" (15:55 KJV). Jesus has shown us all a different way to live—and a different way to encounter death. It has become a doorway into His presence, a portal to something bigger and grander than we could ever imagine.

I think C. S. Lewis may be the author who has managed best to give us an image of the playful joy we may find on the other side of death. At the end of *The Last Battle*, one of Lewis's books about Narnia, Aslan says to the children, "Your father and mother and all of you are—as you used to call it in the Shadowlands—dead. The term is over: the holidays have begun. The dream is ended: this is the morning." Lewis goes on to say:

> For them it was only the beginning of the real story. All their life in this world and all their adventures in Narnia had only been the cover and the title page: now at last they were beginning Chapter One of the Great Story which no one on earth has read: which goes on forever: in which every chapter is better than the one before.

God of all life, I ask that You take away my fear of death. May I face it not so much with courage as with joy. Teach me to smile at the future.

More Than Ready

When my daughter was a preschooler, she dreaded going to kindergarten. She worried about leaving me; she didn't want to have to leave her toys behind at home for the entire day; and she was afraid she wouldn't be big enough to climb up the big steps on the bus. School was a big, unknown place that filled her with fear. She couldn't imagine what it would be like, and she worried that it would be terrible!

By the time the big day came, though, she was more than ready. She put on her new clothes, so excited she was dancing, and then she skipped out to the bus. She never even looked over her shoulder at me as she climbed aboard.

When I think about death, I always think about that moment. Whatever lies on the other side of our dying moments is a big unknown. We can't imagine what it will be like; we can only imagine this world and the joys we have here. When we think of leaving them behind, we feel such sorrow and fear that it hardly seems we can bear it. Death looks dark and grim. Actually, though, death is only dark! It's dark in the sense that we can't see what it holds. But when the time comes for us to go there, we will find that with Christ at our side, we are as ready as my daughter was for kindergarten.

I also imagine that death must be a lot like birth, from the baby's perspective. Imagine if all you had ever known was a small, dark, warm world where your every need flowed into you. If we could somehow send messages to unborn babies, telling them that there was an entire, huge, bright world outside the small, safe space they knew, babies would never be able to imagine what we were talking about. Nothing in their experience would give them the images they would need to picture the enormous world outside their mothers' bodies. If they could understand the day would come when they would have to leave the safety of the womb, that that day was drawing inevitably closer and closer, they might feel a sense of fear, even dread. Why would they want to leave the closeness they had with their mothers? Why would they want to venture out into a cold, vast space filled with new colors, tastes, and sensations? And yet their birthday will arrive, whether they want it to or not—and despite the trauma of birth, they will find they are ready after all for the new life that's ahead. The mother who surrounded them all those months without them every truly comprehending her presence is there, holding them—and they see her face to-face. A world they never could have imagined awaits them.

It's natural to fear the unknown. But as we tap into the strength that the Proverbs 31 woman models for us, we may find that we, too, can face the future with laughter. Our dying days will be as joyful as our birthdays.

Jesus, I know that You await me on the other side of death's door. I am looking forward to seeing You face-to-face.

A World Of Change

It is not only physical death that we fear lies in wait for us in the future. We fear that the future will hold other deaths as well: the death of a valued role, the death of a treasured friendship, the death of our independence, the death of our hopes and dreams.

We live in a world of change. Nothing stays the same, and as each new thing comes into being, something else is put to death. Our tendency is to hold on to the old, the familiar. We hate to let go.

But the natural world gives us resurrection images that can teach our fearful hearts. Would we really want summer to never die? If it were always summer, wouldn't we miss the crisp scarlet and gold days of autumn? Wouldn't we miss the quiet purity of new snow falling on a sleeping world? As we live through these small annual deaths brought about by the turning seasons, we experience each year again the new life of spring, the resurrection joy of daffodils and robin song and creeks wild with melted ice.

When Jesus triumphed over death, it wasn't only physical death that He overcame. He overcame *all* death. He showed us a way to live free from that fear because He put death to death. In every death, Jesus rises up. He shows to us the way of resurrection. "When the perishable puts on the imperishable," Paul wrote in his first epistle to the church at Corinth, "and the mortal puts on immortality, then shall come to pass the saying that is written: 'Death is swallowed up in victory'" (1 Corinthians 15:54 ESV).

216

We might consider for a moment: What is in danger of dying in our lives? Is it our pride? Our happiness? Love? Confidence? Whatever it is, we can claim the assurance that death will never have the last word. Spring always follows even the coldest winters—and the power of the resurrection can never be overcome.

We read in Hebrews: "Because God's children are human beings—made of flesh and blood—the Son also became flesh and blood. For only as a human being could he die, and only by dying could he break the. . . power of death" (2:14 NLT). Jesus experienced death for Himself—and then He won the victory over it.

As impossible as it sometimes seems, we, too, can experience this victory. We read in the book of Revelation, "Blessed and holy is the one who shares in the first resurrection! Over such the second death has no power" (20:6 ESV). When we die to ourselves— when we surrender ourselves to Christ, following His model of life and love—we no longer need to fear the presence of death in our lives. Our ideas about the very nature of death—any sort of death—will change. We will be able to look at it with a smile on our face.

Jesus, thank You for being willing to die so that I no longer have to fear the presence of death. When fears beset me, remind me to fix my eyes on You.

A New Outlook

In the days before my father died, he would often say, "Why should I be afraid of dying? Everything in life that I ever feared turned out to be okay. If life is so filled with beauty, why would I think death would be any different? God has never failed me once in my life. Why would He fail me now?"

Not many of us have this outlook. Instead of basing our expectations for the future on the joys and wonders we have already encountered, we expect the future to be full of pain. We imagine how awful it will be. We brace ourselves for countless disasters.

But most of those disasters will never happen. Yes, we will all ultimately die, in one way or another—but in between that day and today is a space that God has filled with blessings. Yes, we may die in an accident next year, but it's no more likely to happen in the future than it is to happen right now. And yet we feel as though because we can see the present moment, we have control over it (though of course we don't), and because we can't see the future, we feel out of control.

Humans don't like to feel powerless. We imagine that by picturing future dangers we will somehow have more control over them. Instead, as we anticipate future pain (which may never happen), we allow it to rob us of the joy of the present moment. We're so busy with imaginary sorrow and pain that we miss out on the comfort and security that surround us today. We make ourselves miserable for no *real* reason!

The Proverbs 31 woman, however, was not afraid

of the unknown. Her willingness to try new things may have been one of the things that made her able to laugh as she faced the future. She had practice at venturing into the unknown, and like my father, she based her confidence in the future on her experience in the past. God had never failed her, and she knew He never would. Secure in His love, she could embrace the unknown, even take joy in it. For her the future was an adventure. Instead of expecting nothing but loss and pain, she could laugh, anticipating new joys.

The fear of the unknown is natural, and we need not feel guilt over it. We don't need to pretend our fear isn't there or try to squash it out of existence. Instead, we can look at it honestly. We can accept it, even learn from it.

God doesn't think we're sinning if we worry about the future! But He does long to relieve us of this heavy burden we carry so needlessly. "For I know the plans I have for you," He says to us in the book of Jeremiah, "plans for welfare and not for evil, to give you a future and a hope" (29:11 ESV). If the Creator of the universe has a plan for our future lives, why wouldn't we be filled with joy?

Lord, I give You my fears about the future. Thank You that no matter what the future holds, I can count on Your continued presence and blessings in my life.

Turning Points

I am facing a time in my life when it seems that many of the things I have counted on have ended or are coming to an end. My children are moving into a different stage of life where they no longer need me in the same way—and that means my identity as a mother has changed. An old friendship has ended painfully, and there seems to be nothing I can do to mend it. I am in the midst of a major professional change, and it requires a shift in my understanding of my roles. Both my parents have recently died, which means that my identity as their daughter seems to have disappeared. Surrounded by so much change, I'm not sure what the future will hold. I'm not even sure of my own identity anymore! It feels like I'm in the midst of a crisis—and I am.

Psychologists, however, tell us that we don't *have* to define periods of drastic change in our lives as catastrophes, even though they may indeed be crises. The Greek root word for "crisis" means "turning point." When we are going through major upheavals in our lives, we are truly facing a turning point. We are, in fact, going through a transformation. We are entering a new phase of our lives. It will mean we have to let go of many things—but it will also bring new growth to our hearts and souls.

During these turning-point times, we may no longer know how to respond to questions whose answers once came to us so automatically, questions like:

Who am I?

What is my purpose in life?

What do I need to be content?

What is God asking of me?

Without our old familiar answers to those questions, we no longer know who we are. We feel lost.

The temptation is to rush out and snatch answers, any answers, just so we can regain our footing in life. We might plunge into a new job that's as much like our old job as we can find. If we've lost an important relationship, we may try to find another that's similar to what we've lost. We don't like the sense that something essential is missing from our lives, so we try to re-create the past. We can't, of course, and our attempts to do so are often disastrous.

We can choose, instead, to face the future that's speeding toward us with curiosity. What will our new lives reveal to us about God, ourselves, and life? How will we be asked to grow? What new people, places, and ideas will we encounter?

I can imagine the gladness on the Proverbs 31 woman's face as she headed into the wild winds of change. Her delight in whatever was coming was possible because she held within her an inner steadiness. She could encounter changes in her external roles fearlessly because she trusted the One who knew the secret of her deepest identity—even when she didn't.

Paul tells us in 1 Corinthians 6:17, "The person who unites himself with the Lord becomes one spirit with him" (ISV). When the future threatens to strip away our current identities, we may be thrown off balance, but we, too, will have an inner steadiness if we have joined our deepest selves with Christ. Our "real life is hidden with Christ in God" (Colossians 3:3 NLT).

Dear Lord, help me to always turn to You for my identity. Give me the inner steadiness I need to face the changes in my life. Hide my life in You.

Make Time For The Sunshine

When we face the future, sometimes all we see ahead are gray days. With all the responsibilities and troubles in life, we may feel as though we'd be immature and shallow to even dream of sunny days. Sunshine is for kids, we think; grown-up life is *serious*.

God is there with us in our shadows, of course—but He also made the sunshine, and He wants to share it with us. He wants us to remember that even the dreariest, darkest winters yield way to spring. And when the sun comes out, He doesn't want us to miss it! He calls us to come outside, to play, to laugh, to have a child's heart again. He shouts to us, "Come out of your dark house where you've been hiding, brooding over your worries. Come play!"

We may find we can face the future with a greater sense of childlike joy and curiosity when we literally go outside into the outdoor world. Sometimes we get so busy with our gloomy, grown-up, indoor lives that when we finally step outside, we're surprised to find the sun is actually shining after all. We need to take these occasional breaks; we need to make time for sunshine. The sun's warmth on our faces will bring us a new sense of well-being and hope. The future will no longer look so bleak.

Pessimism—expecting only bad things to happen—is not an accurate way to look at the world. The sunny side of life is every bit as real and valuable as life's gray days. God has things He longs to share with us in the sunshine, and He wants to see us smile.

The world may tell us that taking time for

pleasure, laughter, and play is irresponsible. It insists that we have to be *productive* in some way, every minute that we're awake. We don't have time for the sort of joy that children take for granted. No matter how much we rush, no matter how busy we are, no matter how frantically we hurry from one task to another, we can never get caught up. And meanwhile, the years keep going by, and we keep getting older and older. The minutes of our lives are like coins that slip away from our grasp all too quickly.

But it's not the years that make us old. Instead, we get old when responsibilities loom larger than joys, when we lose our sense of humor, when we forget how to play. We're too busy for such foolishness. . .and our hearts begin to wrinkle and our spiritual shoulders stoop. The sun goes behind the clouds, and everywhere we look we see only shades of gray.

As Christ's followers, however, we can refuse to grow old. Instead, we can seek out the delight that life has to offer, even in the midst of pain and trouble. We can take time to laugh, to play, to rejoice in all God has given us. The future will no longer seem so dark.

A child throwing coins into a fountain doesn't care if she's wasting money. She knows only that she's having fun—and by doing so she spreads her joy. We can be the same with life's pleasures. We don't have to worry about wasting time. Time is one of God's gifts to us, and we need not be afraid to spend it. Instead, we can make room in our lives for delight. We can take time to sit in the sun, smiling as we dream about the future.

Jesus, teach me to play again. Lighten my heart.
Fill me with a child's joyful curiosity.

Women Of Hope

Sometimes it seems easier to face the future with fear rather than hope. We feel as though if we brace ourselves for the worst, we can be ready for it. But God wants us to be women of hope, not fear.

It's only natural to fear the unknown, to feel anxiety as we face the future. Four-year-olds often fear kindergarten; children sometimes fear adulthood; and adults fear major life changes like a move across the country, a new job, or other new responsibilities. We fear old age. And death is the ultimate fear.

When we look back, though, we usually find that when the change we dreaded actually arrived, we were ready for it—and it brought us greater freedom, greater satisfaction, greater happiness than what we had experienced before. The eight-year-old is not ready for the responsibilities of adulthood—but the twenty-two-year-old revels in them; and the new job or new home that filled us with anxiety brings with it new friends and new accomplishments that fulfill us in ways we never imagined. Old age has special rewards of its own—and death, that great unknown, will lead us into the presence of God.

Suzanne Segerstrom is a psychologist who has studied the differences between people who face the future with hope—optimists—and those who face the future with fear—pessimists. Optimists, she found, tend to deal with problems head-on. Instead of walking away, they plan a course of action, seek advice from others, and stay focused on solutions. Even when they don't get the good outcome they'd hoped for, they find ways to learn and grow from the negative experience. As Christ's followers, during hard times we have the same comfort the psalmist had: "Our soul waits for the LORD; he is our help and our shield" (Psalm 33:20 ESV).

Orthodox Jews frequently say this prayer as part of their services: "I believe with perfect faith in the coming of the Messiah; and even though he may tarry, nevertheless, I wait each day for his coming." Despite generations of exile and persecution, they claim this hope, this state of expectant readiness. As Christians, followers of the Messiah, Jesus Christ, we have reason to be confident. We can look toward the future with hope and expectation, excited about what God will do for us each and every new day. With the psalmist we can say, "I look behind me and you're there, then up ahead and you're there, too—your reassuring presence, coming and going. This is too much, too wonderful—I can't take it all in!" (139:5-6 MSG). It's so wonderful we may just burst out laughing.

Lord of joy, fill me with Your hope. May I wait in joyful expectation for whatever You unfold in my life next.

PART XVI

She speaks with wisdom,
and faithful instruction is on her tongue.
—VERSE 26 NIV

Wise Words

In this verse we see again the connection our woman has with wisdom. Wisdom guides her words when she speaks. In the Hebrew, the literal meaning of this verse is this: "She opens her mouth in wisdom and the teaching of kindness is on her tongue." I think maybe this is my favorite of all the descriptions we've read about this woman. I truly want to be like her, wise in my words, teaching kindness to everyone I speak to.

We may have a somewhat foggy understanding of exactly what wisdom is. We know it's not the same as intelligence, and neither is it equivalent to knowledge. It's something deeper and different. A person who lacks both intelligence and knowledge can still be very wise.

The Bible's usage of the word may add to our understanding. When Proverbs 24:3 tells us, "By wisdom a house is built, and by understanding it is established" (ESV), we can understand that wisdom is creative and that its creativity continues on after something has been begun, strengthening the structure. Another implication of this verse might be that wisdom will form a shelter under which we can dwell in safety. We learn in Ecclesiastes 9:16 that wisdom is better than strength. The apostle Paul refers to the wisdom that is the "mystery of God" (1 Corinthians 2:7), and in James 3:17 we read, "But the wisdom from above is first pure, then peaceable, gentle, open to reason, full of mercy and good fruits, impartial and sincere" (ESV). Wisdom, then, is closely connected to kindness. It seems to have a lot in common with love.

What would it mean if we taught kindness every time we opened our mouths? We would no longer snap at our children or complain to our husbands. We wouldn't gossip about our friends (or our enemies). We would be sensitive to others' feelings. We would affirm the people around us, letting them know they are loved and valued. Our children, who so often imitate us, would learn to speak in the same way. Kindness for their friends and siblings would spill out of their mouths. Our friends would start to pick up on this different way of communication. Wisdom and kindness would spread out from us in ever-widening circles.

It sounds impossible. We know how easily cross words fall from our lips. We recognize how much pleasure we take in gossiping. It's hard to believe that we could form new habits of speaking. Even if we tried our best to imitate the Proverbs 31 woman, we would end up saying with Paul, "I want to do what is good, but I don't. I don't want to do what is wrong, but I do it anyway" (Romans 7:19 NLT).

We are not perfect people. We will never be as totally strong and wonderful as the Proverbs 31 woman. But that doesn't mean we can't try to walk in her footsteps, encouraged and inspired by her example. And like Paul, we can take comfort in the fact that even though "evil is right there with me," we can also say, "In my inner being I delight in God's law" (Romans 7:21–22 NIV).

God of love, may I live so close to You that I absorb Your wisdom and kindness—and then I won't have to try so hard to guard my tongue because wisdom and kindness will just naturally spill out of me whenever I talk.

The Power Of A Word

Words have great power. In Genesis, God spoke the world into being, and we, too, have the power to shape the world with our words. We can use words to heal or to harm. Frederick Buechner wrote, "In Hebrew, the word *dabar* means both word and deed. A word doesn't merely say something, it does something. It brings something into being. It makes something happen." Our words also have the power to make things happen.

We can use words to destroy our sense of who we are when we tell ourselves again, "I'm just a failure. I'll never succeed." When we shout unkind words at our husbands, we damage their hearts and confidence. If we say impatient words to our children, we can injure their self-concepts. Bill Gillham wrote, "Verbalizing to a child that he is stupid, ugly, clumsy, uncoordinated, lazy. . .and so on gives him solid evidence that he really *is* a loser." If a child is told she is lazy often enough, she will believe it's an accurate description of her identity. Eventually, what she thinks she is will be what she becomes. Proverbs 23:7 tells us what a person thinks in her heart, so she is. Our words help to create the very reality we've been complaining about. We may not speak profanities or utter crude words, but in reality we may be speaking curses as we talk.

Frederick Buechner wrote, "Words spoken in deep love or deep hate set things in motion within the human heart that can never be reversed." Just as we can use our words to destroy and hurt, words of love have the power to build and heal. Speaking hopeful words to ourselves will make us feel more hopeful. When we tell ourselves, "Give that a try. Even if you fail, it won't be the end of the world—and you might just succeed," we empower ourselves to try new things. Our words give our hearts courage. When we tell our husbands and children that we love them and when we speak to them with kindness and respect, they grow more secure and confident. They are able to treat others with greater kindness, too, and they have the strength they need to confront their lives' challenges. Now we are speaking blessings instead of curses.

The Bible takes the quality of our speech very seriously. "There is one whose rash words are like sword thrusts," says Proverbs 12:18, "but the tongue of the wise brings healing" (ESV). Proverbs 15:4 tells us, "A gentle tongue is a tree of life, but perverseness in it breaks the spirit" (ESV). "Do not let any unwholesome talk come out of your mouths," Paul wrote to the Ephesians, "but only what is helpful for building others up according to their needs, that it may benefit those who listen" (4:29 NIV). "Those who guard their mouths and their tongues keep themselves from calamity," we're told in Proverbs 21:23 (NIV).

The challenge to guard our words is one we must take seriously. We must daily strive to be like the Proverbs 31 woman, speaking only words of wisdom and kindness.

Lord, remind me to use my words to bless and not curse.

Truth And Love

The apostle Paul wrote that when we reach "the whole measure of the fullness of Christ. . .we will no longer be infants, tossed back and forth by the waves. . . . Instead, speaking the truth in love, we will grow to become in every respect the mature body of him who is the head, that is, Christ" (Ephesians 4:13-15 NIV). This verse speaks to that same inner stability we saw earlier in the Proverbs 31 woman. The presence of Christ in the very core of our being acts the way a gyroscope does inside a ship, providing equilibrium even when the waves of life—including the changes that come with the passage of time—are wild and stormy. This verse from Ephesians also makes clear the connection between that deep spiritual balance and our ability to speak with wisdom and kindness (what Paul refers to as "speaking the truth in love").

Speaking the truth in love doesn't always come naturally for most of us. It takes discipline and practice. Practice makes all things come more easily. It wears a groove of habit that we can follow better than we can when we are trying out new and unfamiliar behaviors. Repetition brings skill.

Ultimately, however, the ability to consistently speak with truth and love, wisdom and kindness, comes not from skill but from motive. When we are full of resentment or jealousy, it's much harder to speak lovingly. When selfishness is rampant inside us, we are more likely to speak from the desire to manipulate or hurt. Our words tend to reflect what's inside us. We need the inner presence of Christ.

At the same time, however, the more we speak love, the more love will shape our inner hearts. As we've already said, our words have power to shape reality; they can call things into being, even within our own being.

This doesn't mean we say one thing while thinking another, motivated by the desire to deceive or manipulate. We're not pretending to be something we're not in order to impress others. However, we can choose to commit to love, despite the shifting tides of emotion within our hearts. We can make up our minds to use our words to heal and affirm rather than as weapons to hurt or give us power. This takes a clear-eyed, unemotional commitment to truth and love, no matter how we *feel*. It means saying, "I choose love even when I'm angry. I choose truth even when it costs me. I choose kindness even when I'm tired and irritable. I choose wisdom even when I'm exhausted and confused."

Speaking with kindness and love doesn't mean that we always stroke others' egos, either. Many of us are people-pleasers who hate to upset people in any way. Sometimes, however, loving truth may not be easy to hear. Again, we must look carefully at our motivations. Do we hate to upset people with the truth because it makes *us* upset? If that's the case, then we're motivated more by selfishness than compassion. Are we confronting someone out of genuine love? Or do we have a hidden motive (maybe even hidden from our awareness), one that hopes to make someone look bad while we look good? As Jesus recommended, we may need to remove the boards in our own eyes before we can get to work on the splinters in our friends' eyes (Luke 6:42).

Help me, Jesus, to speak with Your love, even when it's hard to do. Give me wisdom to know the right words to speak. Live in me, I pray, so that You can speak through me.

Deeper Meaning

We often don't take our speech seriously enough. We dismiss gossip as a small and understandable habit. Many of us tell small lies automatically, as a way to smooth over social situations. When we're angry, we feel justified using loud words to vent our feelings.

Cultures earlier in human history—cultures we often consider more "primitive"—had a better understanding of words' power. The belief in "magic spells" was not based on the Disney World type of magic we might imagine now but on the very real power of using words to curse or bless. To know someone's true name was once a way of having power over that person, because names—words—had the power not only to identify but also to reveal deeper meaning.

Jewish history includes this perspective on names. The power of names is a thread that runs through the Old Testament, starting with Genesis, where after creating the wild animals and birds, God "brought them to the man to see what he would name them; and whatever the man called each living creature, that was its name" (2:19 NIV). When God changed Abram's name to Abraham and Sarai's name to Sarah (Genesis 17:5, 15), He showed that names were important to the meaning of a person's identity. A twentieth-century Jew, Elie Wiesel, had this to say about names: "In Jewish history, a name has its own history and its own memory. It connects beings with their origins."

In the New Testament, names are still clearly

important. Jesus gave His disciple Simon the name of Peter. The meaning of the new name was "rock," and this would be important to the man's identity within the church. When Saul became a new person in Christ, his name changed to Paul; the man who had been known as a persecutor of Christians now had an entirely new identity as an apostle and leader of the church.

What's interesting is that names sometimes have the power to bring out new facets of a person's being. When Jesus changed Simon's name to Peter, this disciple still wasn't very rocklike. He would let circumstance and fear drive him to denying his Lord. And yet Jesus saw in Peter something that was deeper and truer than his outer behavior. By affirming what He saw, Jesus helped Peter become something more. His new name helped him to find the person God had always intended him to be.

Names and naming were important to the children's author Madeleine L'Engle. She described "Naming" as the power to both reveal and create identity. She described the forces of evil this way: "War and hate are their business, and one of their chief weapons is un-Naming—making people not know who they are. If someone knows who he is, really knows, then he doesn't need to hate." This concept of naming has much in common with the Proverbs 31 woman's words of wisdom and kindness.

What are we naming in our lives? Are we using our words to work hand in hand with God's mission to reveal love through His creation? Or do our words "un-Name"—do they damage others' awareness of God's presence in their lives? This is an important question, a question we need to consider seriously each day. We might even want to start making a practice of hesitating before we speak, to be certain that the words that are about to come out will be words of truth and love. As James writes, "Everyone should be quick to listen, slow to speak" (1:19 NIV).

Help me, Lord, to set a guard over my tongue. May I use my words to always affirm Your love, Your truth, Your wisdom, and Your kindness.

PART XVII

She watches over the affairs of her household
and does not eat the bread of idleness.
—VERSE 27 NIV

Effective Work

By now, we already know that our friend is not lazy! So it comes as no surprise that she doesn't "eat the bread of idleness." Not many of us have the luxury of eating that bread either, so it may be tempting to skip over this verse, thinking to ourselves, *Well, at least I've got that covered!* We would probably feel a little resentful if anyone suggested we needed to consider this verse more carefully. "What *more* can I do?" we might ask.

But we in fact might need to reconsider what this verse is actually saying. Avoiding idleness is *not* the same thing as constantly working. Instead, "eating idleness" means we allow time to be consumed in unproductive ways. And we've all been guilty of that!

When we look at God, we see the divine model for effective work—and the Bible makes clear that it includes rest. Hebrews 4:10 tells us, "For anyone who enters God's rest also rests from their works, just as God did from his" (4:10 NIV).

Entering God's rest means that we take time to allow Him to restore and refresh our minds, bodies, and souls. It doesn't mean we are "wasting time," because this time of renewal is essential to effective work. What's more, when we enter into God's rest, we can also enter the stream of His ongoing work of creation.

This takes away a lot of the weary effort that our lives seem to demand. We might imagine that instead of exhausting ourselves by rowing against life's contrary currents, we're like a boat floating along in the flow of God's work that He has already set in motion. We are in a stream of creative power that is greater than anything we could ever produce on our own.

And within this current, we can both work and rest. We no longer have to feel stressed, knowing that our own strength is unequal to the tasks we've set ourselves. Instead, we can trust the river to carry us along, even when we're resting. We learn to trust God's strength instead of our own. We let divine energy work through us.

Now when we take time to rest, it has nothing to do with being idle, a word that means "empty, worthless," for this is valuable time, time full of meaning. In fact, if we look at our work with this meaning in mind, we might have to admit that we are indeed "eating the bread of idleness," since at least some of our busyness accomplishes very little. If we think about when a car's motor is idling, we may expand our understanding a little further: according to the Oxford Dictionary, an idling motor is "running slowly and steadily without transmitting power." If we're honest, aren't there days when we do an awful lot of running that doesn't transmit power?

The bread of idleness is truly junk food. It's the sort of food that appears appealing but does very little to truly nourish; it fails to give us the health, strength, and energy we need to do God's work.

Lord Jesus, may my time be Your time, my work Your work.
Let me rest in the flow of Your endless creative energy.
May I not try to sustain my efforts with idleness.

We Are His

The first half of verse 27 tells us something else about the Proverbs 31 woman: she watches over her household.

And so do we—but it's not easy. We're responsible for so much. We're housekeepers, laundresses, interior decorators, counselors, confidants, nurses, cooks, friends, chauffeurs, seamstresses, daughters, costume makers, bookkeepers, volunteers, secretaries, manicurists, shoppers, disciplinarians, neighbors, referees. . .and the list goes on and on. Each of these roles is like another ball we're juggling, desperately trying to keep all the balls spinning smoothly through the air, never letting any drop.

Our responsibilities are often overwhelming—and our relationship with God sometimes seems like one more ball we're trying to juggle, something else we're trying to keep up in the air when all around us balls are tumbling and bouncing. In our minds, spending time with God often gets lumped in with things like keeping up an exercise routine or making an effort to have a healthier diet: they're things we *should* do and we know we'd feel better if we did do them—but we're just so busy.

As modern mothers, we have a few more balls to juggle than the Proverbs 31 woman had. We certainly have to deal with more than most of our mothers and grandmothers and great-grandmothers did—things like professions, "quality time" with our children, and the responsibility for aging parents who may live hours away instead of around the block. But women have been jugglers down through the ages—and running a household has always been an exhausting and demanding job. (Think about a world without supermarkets or plastic bags, vacuum cleaners or refrigerators!)

One of my mother's earliest memories is hearing her mother ask their pastor, "How can a woman with four young children and a house to keep possibly find time for prayer?" My grandmother was always considered a "saint," so my mother remembers being astonished to hear genuine anger and frustration in her voice. And when the pastor was unable to find an answer for her, Grandmother turned away with tears in her eyes. I remember my grandmother well: she really wanted to be perfect!

This story took place sixty years ago. But as a Christian wife and mother, I can relate today to my grandmother's frustration and guilt. I think now more than ever, mothers (and particularly Christian mothers) feel called to meet our many roles with saintly perfection—and when we fail to keep all those many balls spinning smoothly and perfectly, we feel as though we have failed, not only physically but spiritually. And none of us likes failure.

But God uses even our failures. He doesn't call us to be perfect; He simply calls us to be *His*.

Loving God, when I've dropped all the balls in my life,
remind me that Your love is never conditional.
You love me just as much when I feel like
a failure. In Your eyes, I am already perfect!

Coming And Going

The Hebrew words in verse 27 have this literal meaning: "She keeps careful watch—like a guard or a watchman—over the comings and goings in her house."

We modern mothers do the exact same job! We keep track of our families' busy schedules. We make sure everyone is where he or she is supposed to be on time. We keep the family on track, and we do all we can to be sure that each family member has what he or she needs—the correct clothing, footwear, food, homework, permission slips, and transportation arrangements—for coming and going.

We don't have any way of knowing exactly how the Proverbs 31 woman managed her busy household, but family time-management experts today suggest several tips that will make this enormous responsibility a little easier. Here's one: keep your family's separate schedules organized. To do this, you'll need a large calendar that has plenty of space for jotting down appointments and commitments for each member of the family. You might use a calendar on your phone or computer, but a large paper or whiteboard calendar that can be posted in the kitchen or some other place is really better. You want to encourage others in the family to consult the calendar for themselves as often as possible, so that they can begin to take on some of the responsibility for remembering where they're supposed to be when.

Don't try to keep separate calendars for separate

family members; each person's schedule really needs to be combined with everyone else's. Otherwise, you may overlook the fact that the day when your husband has promised to pick up the kids after school turns out to be the same day as his dentist appointment. Or you might forget that the special picnic written on your daughter's school schedule requires your presence, meaning that it won't be a good day for you to have a meeting with your team at work.

To make it easier for each person to spot his or her own schedule, you might want to use a different color pen or marker for each individual—but encourage family members not to pay attention *only* to their own schedules. Your household will run more smoothly if you all have some awareness of where you can expect the others to be at the same time.

Next, you need to get in the habit of *immediately* jotting on the calendar (before you forget) *everything* that's coming up that has a specific time or deadline. This will include the obvious things like school holidays, birthdays, sports games, recitals, doctor appointments, and vacations. You'll add to that business meetings, big homework assignments, project deadlines, family gatherings, and church commitments.

As you make your calendar, consider praying with the psalmist, "My times are in your hands" (Psalm 31:15 NIV).

Dear Jesus, You know how busy my household is.
Help me to watch over our comings and goings
with wisdom and love. Keep me organized, I pray.

Time Management

Time-management experts have more good advice to help us watch over our families' busy schedules with all the wisdom and efficiency of the Proverbs 31 woman. Here's another pointer: before you add something new to your family calendar, take a careful look at what's already there. Planning ahead for hectic days can ease some of the stress that comes with managing a family schedule. If you're planning a family gathering, for example, you need to take into consideration the big work project that will be absorbing lots of your time and energy; then you can work around it, instead of setting yourself up for an exhausting week of juggling office work, grocery shopping, and extra housecleaning and cooking. We don't always have any control over the way things pile up on the same day. Your boss may give you a deadline that is the same week that your kids will be needing extra help preparing for finals; the vacation Bible school where you've promised to teach may get rescheduled for the week your husband has to be out of town and your son has to be at baseball camp every day on the other side of town. Some schedule conflicts can be avoided, however, and even the ones that can't will go more smoothly and seem a little less stressful if we've planned for them ahead of time. If you need to free up time on the family calendar, first assess priorities. Consider the importance of certain events to the people involved and any cost (whether monetary or emotional) that might result from canceling.

Make it a daily habit to check your calendar in the morning. Amid the rush of getting ready for the day ahead, it's easy to forget after-school events and appointments. Make another habit of taking a few minutes on the weekends to look at the week ahead. If you see an overloaded day coming up, you'll have more time to shift activities or arrange for carpooling or babysitters. When we leave planning until the last minute or we get caught unprepared because we forgot something, we end up more stressed out.

God has called us to be stewards of His creation. We often apply that idea to our financial affairs, but we sometimes forget that stewardship has to do with our time as well. In fact, the literal meaning of the Greek word often translated in our Bibles as "stewardship" is actually "management of household affairs." Managing a household will always require that we think about time. Keeping the family schedule organized may not seem like a particularly spiritual task—and yet it is one to which we are called by God.

Besides, managing our time more smoothly decreases stress levels and adds peace to our family lives. And that's always a good thing!

God, I ask that You be the Lord of my family's days.
Be with us each hour, each minute.
I entrust our time to You.

Ask For Help

As much as we want to be as competent as the Proverbs 31 woman, there are times when all the many pieces of our household lives seem to slip out of our fingers. When that happens, there are other strategies we may need to consider.

We may need to ask for help. We need to let go of the false pride that wants to impress others with our perfection. It's okay to admit that we don't have things completely under control! Most of our friends and family will understand; even the most organized person is lying if she says she's never been overwhelmed with her life's demands. As the body of Christ, we're meant to offer help to the other members of the body. While one member's schedule is so full she can barely breathe, another member may be at the point in her life where she has time to lend. Your turn to help may come later. It's all part of being part of the body's web of giving and receiving.

A few other household-management strategies may help us as well: don't automatically expect things of yourself that you wouldn't expect of any other member of the family. As we organize the family calendar, we need to look at who is responsible for accomplishing what. Are you doing all the transporting, while another person (one with a driver's license) happens to have ample free time in his schedule at the same time? If you have a large project coming up the same week that you promised to send cookies to school with your son, is he old enough to try his hand at baking his own cookies? Or instead of you spending an evening baking, could your husband pick up something at the grocery store or bakery?

Evaluate your resources, and strategize ways to utilize them efficiently. If your neighbor's daughter is on the same soccer team as yours, maybe you could trade carpooling days. If your parents live nearby and are hinting that they'd like to spend more time with their grandchildren, would they be willing to commit to being with the kids one afternoon a week so that you can take time for an exercise class? In case of an emergency that comes up when both your husband and you are truly unavailable, do you have a friend who can be on standby?

Be realistic. When managing a family schedule, remember that there are only twenty-four hours in a day. If you cram too many activities and commitments into *every* day, you will be adding stress to your lives that's not really necessary. After-school sports practice, ballet lessons, Scouts, and band rehearsals may seem like really good things—but it's impossible to do everything. Teach your children to prioritize. Talk with them about what they would enjoy most; what would they be able to make a long-term commitment to?

Schedule free time, both for yourself and for your family as a whole. When you have time to relax together, your relationships will be nourished. And try to make sure you eat dinner together more nights than you don't! Communication—the sort of conversation that can take place around the dinner table—is crucial to your family's peace and love.

And remember the wisdom that John Lennon learned: in the end, "life is what happens when you're busy making other plans." Be willing to throw your schedule out the window if that's what love asks. Your children's and husband's needs—and yours—are sometimes more important than being on time!

Lord, give me the wisdom to know what is truly important
in my family's life—and then give me the discipline
to set our priorities accordingly. May our love for
You and for each other always come first.

He'll Carry You

The Proverbs 31 woman makes her busy, efficient life look easy. But no one could be so successful—professionally, spiritually, and as a mother and wife—without resources that supported her own talents and abilities. She couldn't have had her confidence and strength without an undergirding of faith.

A friend of mine likes to tell the story of an old lady who was asked after her first-ever airplane flight, "How was it?"

She gave an exhausted sigh and had to clutch the arm of the person who was talking to her to keep herself from falling over. "It was fine," she said. "But I'm just exhausted now."

"Why?" asked her friend. "Couldn't you sleep on the flight?"

"Of course not!" the lady snapped. "I didn't dare ever let my full weight down on the seat."

Obviously, the airplane carried the woman from point A to point B—but she arrived needlessly exhausted. The plane was perfectly capable of carrying her without any effort on her part. In fact, her effort did absolutely nothing; it didn't add the least bit of help to the power of the plane's engines. She could have simply relaxed and enjoyed the flight.

As women, we often have the same attitude toward our lives. We don't trust God's ability to carry our families and ourselves. We think we have to do it for Him.

The metaphor only goes so far, of course. God

expects us to use our talents and abilities; He works through our work. But at another level, we all need to comprehend that even when our own efforts seem to be failing, we are still being carried forward. We need to remember that Jesus told us, "Come to me, all of you who are weary and carry heavy burdens, and I will give you rest" (Matthew 11:28 NLT). We can come to God and give Him all our worries and cares, knowing that He truly cares about the events of our lives (1 Peter 5:7). We don't need to be like God's people who refused His help in Isaiah, so that He said to them, "Only in returning to me and resting in me will you be saved. In quietness and confidence is your strength. But you would have none of it" (30:15 NLT).

Other translations of the Bible use the word *repentance* in this verse from Isaiah instead of "returning to me." We often connect repentance with "more serious" sins than trying to do things for ourselves, but God wants to readjust our thinking. He wants us to turn to Him even in the smallest details of our lives. He longs to carry us.

Thank You, Lord of heaven and earth, that You are carrying me. If You can keep the stars on course, I know I can trust You with the details of my household's life.

PART XVIII

Her children arise and call her blessed;
her husband also, and he praises her:
"Many women do noble things,
but you surpass them all."
—VERSES 28-29 NIV

Practice Praying

The Proverbs 31 woman's family may have taken her efficiency and strength for granted some of the time— but in the end, they noticed all she did for them. They appreciated who she was and all the ways she blessed them.

Some days, though, we may feel we've been waiting a long time for our family to notice all we do. No one's called us blessed for a long time! It's hard not to feel used and ignored, and resentment and hurt may brim up in our hearts.

When that happens, we might try prayer instead of complaints. I find that when I pray for my family regularly, I am changed. Maybe it's just that prayer opens the door for God to come into my home— and when He does, He puts His creative hand on all the different parts of our family's life. Or maybe it's because prayer allows me to shift my attention away from my own needs.

Sometimes I bring my hurt and resentment to God—and I find my family life works far better when I dump those feelings on God's shoulders rather than on my husband's or my children's. I can be completely honest with God, expressing how angry I really am, and yet gradually, as I pray, I'll find my heart being soothed.

I begin to see things from my husband's perspective as well as my own; I understand my children a little better. When I let go of at least some of my anger, I can see my family more clearly again. I can look at them with the eyes of love, recognizing their needs.

As we see our family members' needs more clearly, we can give them to God as well. Instead of fretting and stewing over them, trying to figure out how *we* can fix things, we can release these needs into God's hands, knowing His hands are big enough to hold them all. When we do, we're free to experience the peace God wants us to have.

When we also practice praying for our family members with thankful hearts, expressing our joy and gratitude for each of them, we will find that we are more aware of their strengths and less focused on our complaints.

Jesus reveals Himself to us through our families, for they are a part of His body on earth. Their hands and smiles, their voices and their grubby little feet, bring Jesus to us—and we have the opportunity and privilege of handing Jesus back to them with our own hands and voices, with each little thing we do for them, no matter how small.

God doesn't ask us to be downtrodden slaves. When we speak the truth in love, we may need to confront family members who are not treating us with the respect or consideration we deserve. But we can ask God to give us the wisdom to address those concerns with kindness.

The word *humility* comes from the same root words as *soil*—and new life springs out of the fertile ground of humility. Meanwhile, pride and self-centered resentment produce nothing in our hearts but dead, dry weeds. When we practice times of prayerful self-examination, we may see the stubborn weeds in our own hearts that are choking our families' lives together. And eventually, our families *will* notice!

Reveal to me, Lord, the areas where I'm at fault—and give me the strength to change.

Instrument Of Peace

While we're waiting for the days when our husbands and children bless us with gratitude and appreciation, we might want to claim the prayer of Francis of Assisi as our own (my additions are in parentheses):

Lord, make me an instrument of thy peace.

Where there is hatred, let me sow love. *(When my children are screaming at each other, may I not add my own voice to the chaos. Instead, give me wisdom to guide them back into harmony with each other.)*

Where there is injury, pardon. *(When my child's feelings have been hurt, may I help her to forgive.)*

Where there is doubt, faith. *(When my husband worries about our finances, may I support him and help him to regain his confidence in Your providence.)*

Where there is despair, hope. *(When my child believes she will never pass her math exam, may I encourage her and give her confidence to do her best.)*

Where there is darkness, light. *(When my husband can't see the way ahead at his job, may I lend my insights to him in a constructive way that will help him gain a new sense of direction.)*

Where there is sadness, joy. (*Show me the way to comfort my child after the death of our beloved pet. Give me the words to bring the smile back to his face.*)

O divine Master, grant that I may not so much seek to be consoled as to console. (*Help me not to hold back my sympathy for my husband's disappointment at work because I don't feel he's been sympathetic enough toward my own work concerns.*)

To be understood as to understand. (*Remind me not to expect my teenager to see my perspective when she's never been a mother or faced an adult's responsibilities—but I have been a teenager, and I can remember what it was like and lend her the benefit of my understanding.*)

To be loved as to love. (*May I not wait to express my love to my husband until he tells me, "I love you"—and in exactly the way I want to be told.*)

For it is in giving that we receive; It is in pardoning that we are pardoned; It is in dying to self that we are born to eternal life.

Family life is not easy. It demands daily small deaths to ourselves, and it offers us countless opportunities to express the love of Christ. It gives us a thousand moments each and every day when we bless and are blessed by the people with whom we share a house.

Beloved God, thank You for my family.
May I be more concerned with blessing them
than I am with their blessing me.

A Radical Shift

We live in a world where we've learned that we can't get something for nothing. Everything comes back to "You scratch my back, I'll scratch yours." We learned the principle when we were very young, on the playground maybe, when some little boy or girl said, "You give me your marbles, and I'll give you my Cracker Jacks." When we grew up, we understood that we wouldn't get far in life—or make any money—if we didn't work hard. Nice clothes and cars and houses— all the good things this world has to offer—cost money, and most of us can only get money if we work for it. We have to earn it.

We tend to carry these hard-won insights into our family lives. Even while we may pray the words of Saint Francis's lovely prayer, we don't realize that our society's perspectives are shaping our actions and attitudes. Loving our families with the love of Christ requires a radical shift in our hearts and behaviors.

We've talked about the healthy give-and-take that circulates like blood through the body of Christ, but it's a far different thing from the scratch-my-back-I'll-scratch-yours attitude that we've all learned. Our culture's perspective says, "I'll give something to you *after* you've given something to me." It's turned backward from what happens inside Christ's body, where we give freely and continuously.

As we bless others in our households, blessing flows back to us naturally, the way our breath goes in and out—but it doesn't work if we think we can control how and when we receive blessing. Christ asks us to love as He loved, without conditions or expectations. A healthy household will experience the normal flow of love, in and out, between its members—but for that to happen, we must surrender our need to be in control. Deep inside us, where we still secretly consider our own needs as more important than anyone else's, we must learn to surrender and simply trust God's love as it flows into us, through us, and out from us.

This readjustment in our thinking challenges us. It will change us, both internally and externally. We will not only relate to our families differently, but also come to God in a new way.

Our assumptions about how relationships work have shaped how we think of God. We assume He works from the same principles we've learned out there in the dog-eat-dog world. Deep in our hearts, we believe we'll have to earn His favor. We think God will only give to us if we give to Him. So we try to be good. We work hard to look like Christians on the outside. We follow all the rules. It's never good enough, of course. No matter how hard we try, we can never make ourselves good.

And it doesn't matter! God turns our human rules upside down. He gives to us when we do absolutely nothing. He gives to us when we don't deserve anything. He gives to us no matter what. Christ's life and death are the embodiment of God's giving nature, His commitment to give absolutely everything to us, no matter how broken we may be. That's grace.

Grace asks nothing of us except trust. It asks us

to let go of our own efforts so that grace can work through us. When we open our hearts, grace will flow into us—and out from us to our families.

God of love, thank You for Your endless, unconditional love and grace. It seems too good to be true! Teach me to believe. Help me to trust. Change me.

Tides Of Love

When we think back to those moments when we first held our babies, we remember the tide of love that flooded through us. If it was our first child, we may have been amazed at the intensity of our feelings. All our body's hormones and our heart's deepest depths flowed together in an enormous flood of love. We knew we would literally die for the small human being in our arms.

In the days that followed, we found that motherhood was not quite the rosy, lovely thing we might have expected it to be. Sleep-deprived and hormonal, we discovered we were not the center of the world as we once supposed. Our needs for comfort and entertainment, for independence and control, all became secondary to another's insistent needs. We were forced to set aside our own clamoring egos so we could care for our babies, who depended on us for their very existence. Willingly or not, we made room in our lives for Christ's love to be born. We emptied ourselves, as He did, and were broken so that another can live.

That love is still there in the background as our children grow. We don't need to think it—or even feel it—to know it's there. At the same time, our love for our children grows bigger and wider. It asks new things of us. They no longer need us to get up in the middle of the night to feed them; instead, as they become teenagers, we wait up at night for them to come home. We don't have to worry about toilet training them anymore; now we're worried about teaching them to drive safely. In some ways motherhood gets easier the older our children become—and in other ways it becomes harder and harder. It demands that we surrender more and more of our control. We have no choice but to let go of these beloved individuals, these people for whom we would still lay down our lives, and allow them to leave us, both physically and emotionally.

Before the power of the resurrection can be born in our lives, wrote William Law, a spiritual writer of the eighteenth century, "there must be some kind of earthquake within us, something that must rend and shake us to the bottom." Motherhood can be that sort of earthquake in our hearts. It will continue to shake and rattle us for the rest of our lives!

Motherhood is an all-the-time job that doesn't end even when our children are grown and independent. Even when they no longer live at home with us, our relationships with them will require that we continue to look ever more deeply into our own hearts. We will be called to die to our egos in new ways.

And God will be with us through it all. As He uses us to bless our children, He will bless us. He loves us even more than we love our children.

Thank You, God, for loving me. Thank You for all You are teaching me through my children. Bless them, please, as much as they bless me.

Walls

We all have walls we've erected around our hearts, walls that are designed to protect our rights, our individuality, our interests. These walls may seem like a necessity in the world in which we live, but the thing about walls is this: they not only protect us, but also keep people—and God—out.

As we live closely within a family household, learning to respect and love others as much as we do ourselves, at first we may find a brick here and there needs to be removed from our carefully constructed walls. As we yield to the Spirit's action in our lives, we find that whole sections wobble and fall. Eventually, as the years go by, like the walls of Jericho, the whole structure comes a-tumbling down. Family life by its very nature demands that those high, selfish walls fall flat. The process is uncomfortable, painful, even terrifying. But God knew all along that it was the only way we could learn to truly love and be loved.

When the walls are down, when our hearts are naked and exposed, God, too, is free to come into our hearts in new and intimate ways.

As mothers, we no longer have the luxury of postponing our spiritual growth for another easier day (a day, for example, when we have more time, a day when we can finally have some peace and quiet all to ourselves). Instead, our family's needs demand that we must somehow recognize Jesus' face in a thousand small and concrete ways. We need to somehow see Him in the midst of dirty diapers and peanut butter sandwiches and quarreling children. We need to feel His presence flowing through hectic schedules, in car pools, in housework and mealtimes, and in our families' faces.

Doing this is often an enormous challenge. Anyone who says it is easy is lying! To help us see more clearly with the eyes of our spirits, we might want to try this exercise now and then to help us see Jesus a little more clearly: become a child again and practice your powers of make-believe. The next time you know a particularly stressful day lies ahead, decide to pretend that Jesus is actually beside you in physical form. As you drive your children to school, picture Him next to you or behind you in the car. While you sit at your desk at work or go about your household chores, imagine that He is right beside you. Not only is He observing your work, but He is also lending a hand.

Allow yourself to talk to Jesus throughout your day. Complain to Him. Laugh with Him. Listen to Him. What is He saying to you?

At the end of the day, look back and evaluate your day. How did imagining Christ's physical presence at your side change your behaviors? How did it affect your emotions?

And the thing about this exercise? It's not just make-believe. Jesus really *is* beside you all day long.

Jesus, thank You for being my companion even on my busiest days. Forgive me when I ignore You. I would never treat another person with such rudeness, and yet I know that's often how I treat You. When that happens, please give me a tap. Remind me that You're there.

Put Love Into Practice

Our family households are the places where each member of the family learns about love. Love may be a spiritual quality—but it's also as down-to-earth and practical as the air we breathe.

As human beings, we need love. In fact, psychologists tell us that love is as necessary to our lives as oxygen. The more connected we are to others and to God, the healthier we will be, both physically and emotionally—and the less connected we are, the more we are at risk.

Our culture tends to believe that love "just happens." If we don't feel enough love in our lives, then we're just not one of the lucky people. But love doesn't work that way. Psychologist Erich Fromm called love "an act of will." To feel love in our lives, we have to make up our minds to act in loving ways. We have to put our love for God and others into practice.

There are concrete ways we do this within our families. Here are some of them:

- Focus on God and your children and husband. Don't obsess about your own concerns. Instead, shift your attention outside yourself. Look at God. Notice the person next to you (whether that's your husband, a child, a friend, a coworker, or a stranger you've met in passing).

- Go out of your way to help someone else. Notice the needs around you—and do something practical to meet them, even in the smallest of ways.
- Practice looking at things from other perspectives besides your own. This could mean something as simple as imagining yourself in your teenager's shoes. It also means truly listening when your child speaks.
- Allow yourself to absorb God's perspective daily, through scripture and prayer.

God's love is never ending. There is nothing we need to do to deserve that love or to draw it to us. But there *are* ways that we can allow that love to flow through us to our families, enabling it to bless their hearts as well as our own.

Thank You, loving God, for my family. Thank You for the love I feel for each member—and thank You for the love they have for me. Use us all, I pray, to teach each other more about You and Your love.

PART XIX

Charm is deceptive, and beauty is fleeting;
but a woman who fears the LORD is to be praised.
Honor her for all that her hands have done,
and let her works bring her praise at the city gate.
—VERSES 30–31 NIV

Proof Of Value

The woman in Proverbs 31 takes care of herself and her appearance—but she also knows that there's more to her than the way she looks. She knows that the way she interacts with others is important—but social skills (or charm) aren't as important as integrity. The best proof of her value is in her actions.

While this is true, we don't need to allow her example to encourage our tendency toward perfectionism. God doesn't demand that we be perfect, and neither do our families.

All too often we are harder on ourselves than anyone else. Now and then, remind yourself to listen to your silent internal dialogue, for instance, the next time you're trying on a bathing suit in a store changing room. What is that little voice saying? Is it pointing out every bulge and dimple? Is its voice harsh and scornful? Now imagine a friend—or your daughter—was the one trying on a bathing suit. Would you brutally list every flaw you see? Would you really even notice? Even if you did, even if that particular bathing suit wasn't a good choice, wouldn't you still focus on the positive as much as possible? Wouldn't you temper your honesty with gentleness and love?

As mothers, most of us know we need to affirm our children and husbands. We're not perfect at it, even with those we love the most, but still our goal is generally to build up our loved ones rather than to tear them down. We need to practice these same skills with ourselves.

You might try this exercise: the next time you feel upset about your appearance or some other aspect of yourself you feel doesn't measure up, treat yourself as gently as you would an anxious child. Try demonstrating to yourself the love described in 1 Corinthians 13, and ask yourself these questions:

- ᴕ Are you patient with yourself?
- ᴕ Are you kind to yourself?
- ᴕ Do you dishonor yourself? Or do you respect yourself?
- ᴕ Do you feel angry with yourself? Or do you forgive yourself for being less than perfect?
- ᴕ Do you keep a record of all the wrong things you've ever done—and remind yourself of them again and again?
- ᴕ Do you protect yourself (in a healthy way)?
- ᴕ Do you trust yourself?
- ᴕ Do you give up on yourself? Or do you keep trying, keep hoping?

Lord, help me to love myself with Your love. Heal my wounds, and make me realize that I am filled with honor because You live within me.

Satisfied

If only I were married, I used to think back in my single days, *then I would be happier*. And then I fell in love and married, and yes, marriage was marvelous—but almost immediately I began to think, *If only we had our own house. . .* And then it was, *If only we could have children. . .* And then, *If only I could achieve this one professional goal. . .*

It's good to have goals; they help us find direction and keep our focus. But we need to remember that these goals cannot provide a true answer to our dissatisfaction with our lives or with ourselves. No matter how hard we work and strive, we will never quite reach the ideal we believe lies waiting just over the horizon. That's not the way to find the strength and serenity of the Proverbs 31 woman.

But we're so seldom satisfied with life, particularly with ourselves. No matter how much we achieve, we always know we have further to go on our endless journey toward perfection. If we're trying to lose weight, for example, when we lose that five pounds we were hoping to drop, instead of taking a moment to pat ourselves on the back, we instantly turn our attention to the *next* five pounds. No wonder we get so exhausted sometimes; no wonder our lives seem like such struggles. We're like thirsty people staggering through the desert toward mirages that constantly retreat.

That's the thing about mirages: we never reach them because they're not real. In reality, each of our days is filled with tiny achievements. We need to recognize them, for little by little they will accumulate. If we will accept only perfection in ourselves and nothing less, we will always be discouraged. Inevitably, we will become frustrated. Eventually, we may give up altogether.

God doesn't want us to follow the mirages of perfection. Instead, His grace gives us strength to walk step by step, delighting in the joys of this present moment, with all its imperfection. He wants us to find delight in being ourselves, now, as we stand in His presence. "My grace is all you need," He reminds us. "My power works best in weakness" (2 Corinthians 12:9 NLT).

Thank You, Lord Jesus, for Your endless grace that asks nothing of me but my surrender to Your love.

Heart-Comforts

As women, we all need encouragement now and then. Here are some words to comfort our hearts and make us smile:

When you are a mother, you are never really alone in your thoughts. A mother always has to think twice, once for herself and once for her child.
—SOPHIA LOREN

You are doing God's work. You are doing it wonderfully well. He is blessing you, and He will bless you, even—no, especially—when your days and your nights may be most challenging. Like the woman who. . .fought her way through the crowd just to touch the hem of the Master's garment, so Christ will say to the women who worry and wonder and weep over their responsibility as mothers, "Daughter, be of good comfort; thy faith hath made thee whole." And it will make your children whole as well.
—JEFFREY HOLLAND

I think every. . .mom probably feels the same thing: You go through big chunks of time where you're just thinking, "This is impossible—oh, this is impossible." And then you just keep going and keep going, and you sort of do the impossible.
—TINA FEY

I remember my mother's prayers and they have always followed me. They have clung to me all my life.

—ABRAHAM LINCOLN

There's no way to be a perfect mother and a million ways to be a good one.

—JILL CHURCHILL

The phrase "working mother" is redundant.

—JANE SELLMAN

It's not easy being a mother. If it were easy, fathers would do it.

—DOROTHY ON *THE GOLDEN GIRLS*

Sometimes, when I want to take on the world, I try to remember that it's just as important to sit down and ask my son how he's feeling or talk to him about life.

—ANGELINA JOLIE

There's no such thing as a supermom. We just do the best we can.

—SARAH MICHELLE GELLAR

Notice that many of these quotes are from modern-day women who are mothers themselves. We have many companions on this road!

Lord, be with all of us who are mothers. Be with those of us who are running businesses—and homes. Be with us who are famous—and those of us who aren't. May all of us bring Your blessing to our children and to the world.

Make Space. . .And Then Wait

The Proverbs 31 woman lived a consecrated life. She was committed, she worked hard, but even more than that, she knew *why* she was working. She knew the deepest secret meaning of her life. Her life was consecrated to something bigger than she was.

To "consecrate" means to make something holy, totally dedicated to God. We may think that it requires a special ritual, but it doesn't. A ritual can be useful because it may help make our consecration real to us, but it's only a tangible metaphor. It's a way to help us understand something that is real but invisible. Baptism is one of those rituals: it expresses something real—our new life in Christ—in an outward form. It makes tangible our consecration to God. Formally dedicating our babies is another way we may use a ritual to express the reality of consecration. At a dedication, we stand up in front of our church community and express our commitment to give our children to God.

But after the ritual comes the time to actually live out the promises we made. We have to express our lives' consecration not only in words and images but also with our actions. In humdrum, ordinary ways, again and again, we have to invite God into our households, into our families, and into our own minds and hearts.

To use another metaphor, think about all you do to prepare for a guest who is coming to your home. You sweep and vacuum and dust; you put fresh sheets on the bed; you straighten and tidy and make sure that your guest will have everything she needs. You are consecrating the room for your guest, setting it aside as a place where she will be welcome. And then you await her coming, the moment when you will welcome her into your home.

When we consecrate our lives to God, we make a space where He will be welcome. We lovingly make room for His presence in our lives. We clear out anything that might otherwise take up that space. We wait for a greater awareness of His presence. When we sense He is with us, we welcome Him gladly. We include Him in our lives.

In the Old Testament, Joshua told the people, "Consecrate yourselves, for tomorrow the LORD will do amazing things among you" (Joshua 3:5 NIV). We, too, can expect our Divine Guest to do amazing things in our lives. All we do is make space for Him and welcome Him—and then wait to see what happens next.

Lord, be the unifying principle at the center of my life,
the thing that makes sense of everything else.
Consecrate my life with Your presence.

Not So Serious

A website called the Network describes what a modern-day Proverbs 31 woman might look like if she were to shape herself according to her society's expectations rather than God's:

> She is beautiful; she can wear her wedding dress 10 years after her wedding. To do this, this beautiful woman exercises 20 minutes each day, making a total of 3 hours per week. She watches her diet, prepares nutritious food. . .and is health conscious. . . .
>
> She keeps up her personal appearance. She is color-analyzed, dresses for success, coordinates, harmonizes, and accessorizes in the latest fashions. She keeps everything laundered, cleaned, and pressed—and does this on a minimum budget. . . .
>
> She is coiffured, manicured, and pedicured in trendy styles. . . . This woman is not only beautiful, but also intelligent. She develops her mind by reading daily newspapers, weekly news magazines, monthly best sellers, and watches TV news to keep up with current national and international events. . . . She is educated, informed, and stays aware by taking continuing education classes. Because she has developed her mind, she is career oriented and works outside the home. . . . If she does not work outside the home she has to do all the volunteer work the "working" women do not have time to do, which can

take just as much time as if she were employed.

This beautiful, intelligent woman also cares about her family and community. In the time that remains she keeps an immaculate house, passing the scrutiny of the most inquisitive neighbor at any moment. Her yard also looks like a country garden with flowerbeds that change with the seasons. She spends quality time with her children, plays with them, helps with homework, attends all school and sports events, taxis their friends, and keeps up their wardrobes while serving them nutritious meals every day (which they always enjoy).

She is involved in community affairs, volunteering for scouts, food bank, and any current charity. . . . And the most amazing thing about this ideal woman is that she does all of this and when she goes to bed at night, she never once says to her husband, "I have a headache."[14]

As this website makes clear, women hold themselves up to impossible standards. No one could ever achieve everything on this list, no more than anyone could do all the things that the Proverbs 31 woman did. There just aren't enough hours in any week to do all that, even if a woman had the physical strength and skills she would need to accomplish it all.

But maybe we women misinterpret what's expected of us. With our fixation on our own need for perfection (all the while aware of our imperfection),

14. Peggy Musgrove, "Time Management Tips for Women in Ministry," http://ag.org/wim/0507/0507_TimeManagement.cfm.

we see every bit of good advice or loving wisdom
as a condemnation. Instead, if we truly believed
in our own dignity and worth, we'd be able to see
descriptions like this as a chance to affirm women's
very real strength, to pick the qualities that match
up best with our own, to apply one or two things
that might make our lives easier—and then shrug our
shoulders, roll our eyes, and laugh out loud at the
silliness of expecting anything else of ourselves.

Teach me to laugh at myself, Lord.
Help me not to take myself quite so seriously.

Extraordinary Beauty

Few of us realize the extraordinary and unique beauty that lies within each of us. We tend to overlook our own special loveliness. We forget that an extraordinary beauty lies within each of us that is uniquely our own. It has very little to do, though, with our outer appearance.

Our beauty may remind us of the Proverbs 31 woman. It may be quieter—or bolder. It could be gentler and simpler—or more assertive and complicated. God never asks us to be exactly like anyone else. He expresses Himself uniquely through each of us. Our own particular forms of beauty are all our own. It has never come before in anyone else, and it will never come again. This unique beauty is the image of God.

The Proverbs 31 woman may be a challenging ideal to live up to, but she is meant to give us a model that's big enough to contain our own particular version of her beauty. We are not asked to measure up to each other's standards; we are not meant to compare ourselves to each other and compete with each other. I cannot play your song, and you cannot play mine. We are gifts from God to one another; we are the songs He sings to us through each other. If we try to pretend to be something we're not, we muffle the voice of God singing through our special skills and talents. If we try to look like everyone else, measuring up to our society's standards of beauty instead of our own one-of-a-kind beauty, we hide His face from each other.

As women, we do have some things in common: we are all stumbling through life, lunging and leaping to catch all the balls in our busy lives, feeling overwhelmed as they bounce and tumble around us. None of us is perfect.

We want to be. What's more, we like immediate gratification; we're easily discouraged when we have to wait for something. If the goal we have in mind (for example, perfection!) doesn't materialize today. . . or next week. . .or even next year, we're certain that means it will never materialize. We'll never change, never grow, never become better at managing our hectic lives with the peace and skill of the Proverbs 31 woman.

But when we start talking to ourselves with these negative words, we might take a look at the natural world, where immense results are often accomplished with immense slowness. Drop by drop and grain by grain, rock is shaped and canyons carved. Slowly, surely, the earth's face is radically changed.

We, too, are being changed with the same slow sureness. We can afford to be patient with ourselves, for we are loved by a patient God. He has all the time in the world to make us completely beautiful, whole and complete as the one-of-a-kind women that we are. In fact, He has eternity.

And so do we.

I love You, Lord, for making me, me. I give You myself. Express Yourself through me. Use me to bring love into the world in a way no other person could do but me.

Prepared For You

One of my favorite quotes about a woman's life was written by Kathleen O'Connell Chesto in a book called *Why Are the Dandelions Weeds?* Whenever I'm discouraged, it brings tears to my eyes even as it lifts my heart.

> *I have a vision of all the women gathered before God on judgment day. The Lord will say to us: "I was hungry and you fed me, thirsty and you gave me a drink, naked and you clothed me, homeless and you sheltered me, imprisoned and you visited me. . . ."*
>
> *And we will interrupt, protesting, "Not I, Lord. When did I see you hungry and feed you?"*
>
> *And the Lord will say: "How could you ask, you of the three-and-a-half-million peanut butter and jelly sandwiches!"*
>
> *"But thirsty, Lord?"*
>
> *"I was in the Kool-Aid line that came in with the summer heat and the flies, and left fingerprints on your walls and mud on your floors, and you gave me a drink."*
>
> *"But naked, Lord, homeless?"*
>
> *"I was born to you naked and homeless, and you sheltered me, first in wombs and then in arms. You clothed me with your love, and spent the next twenty years keeping me in jeans."*
>
> *"But imprisoned, Lord?"*
>
> *"Oh, yes. For I was imprisoned in my littleness*

behind the bars of a crib and cried out in the night, and you came. I was imprisoned inside a twelve-year-old body that was exploding with so many new emotions, I didn't know who I was anymore, and you loved me into being myself. And I was imprisoned behind my teenage anger, my rebellion, and my stereo set, and you waited outside my locked door for me to let you in.

"Now, Beloved, enter into the joy which has been prepared for you for all eternity."[15]

Dear Lord, I pray now for all of us women. May we know that we, too, are clothed in dignity and honor. May we work with eager hands and strong arms, and may we never be afraid to laugh at the future. Give us the courage to try new things and the compassion to give to others from our own resources. Bless our enterprises—all our projects, our professions, our businesses—as well as our homes. May we not spin our wheels uselessly but instead flow in the current of Your love. Use us, I pray, to bless our husbands and children. Give us strength for our busy days. Teach us that we are each truly beautiful because You love us.

---

15. Kathleen Chesto, *Why Are the Dandelions Weeds?* (Kansas City: Sheed & Ward, 1993), 146–47. Used with permission.

Read Thru the Bible in a Year

1–Jan	Gen. 1–2	Matt. 1	Ps. 1
2–Jan	Gen. 3–4	Matt. 2	Ps. 2
3–Jan	Gen. 5–7	Matt. 3	Ps. 3
4–Jan	Gen. 8–10	Matt. 4	Ps. 4
5–Jan	Gen. 11–13	Matt. 5:1–20	Ps. 5
6–Jan	Gen. 14–16	Matt. 5:21–48	Ps. 6
7–Jan	Gen. 17–18	Matt. 6:1–18	Ps. 7
8–Jan	Gen. 19–20	Matt. 6:19–34	Ps. 8
9–Jan	Gen. 21–23	Matt. 7:1–11	Ps. 9:1–8
10–Jan	Gen. 24	Matt. 7:12–29	Ps. 9:9–20
11–Jan	Gen. 25–26	Matt. 8:1–17	Ps. 10:1–11
12–Jan	Gen. 27:1–28:9	Matt. 8:18–34	Ps. 10:12–18
13–Jan	Gen. 28:10–29:35	Matt. 9	Ps. 11
14–Jan	Gen. 30:1–31:21	Matt. 10:1–15	Ps. 12
15–Jan	Gen. 31:22–32:21	Matt. 10:16–36	Ps. 13
16–Jan	Gen. 32:22–34:31	Matt. 10:37–11:6	Ps. 14
17–Jan	Gen. 35–36	Matt. 11:7–24	Ps. 15
18–Jan	Gen. 37–38	Matt. 11:25–30	Ps. 16
19–Jan	Gen. 39–40	Matt. 12:1–29	Ps. 17
20–Jan	Gen. 41	Matt. 12:30–50	Ps. 18:1–15
21–Jan	Gen. 42–43	Matt. 13:1–9	Ps. 18:16–29
22–Jan	Gen. 44–45	Matt. 13:10–23	Ps. 18:30–50
23–Jan	Gen. 46:1–47:26	Matt. 13:24–43	Ps. 19
24–Jan	Gen. 47:27–49:28	Matt. 13:44–58	Ps. 20
25–Jan	Gen. 49:29–Exod. 1:22	Matt. 14	Ps. 21
26–Jan	Exod. 2–3	Matt. 15:1–28	Ps. 22:1–21
27–Jan	Exod. 4:1–5:21	Matt. 15:29–16:12	Ps. 22:22–31
28–Jan	Exod. 5:22–7:24	Matt. 16:13–28	Ps. 23

29–Jan	Exod. 7:25–9:35	Matt. 17:1–9	Ps. 24
30–Jan	Exod. 10–11	Matt. 17:10–27	Ps. 25
31–Jan	Exod. 12	Matt. 18:1–20	Ps. 26
1–Feb	Exod. 13–14	Matt. 18:21–35	Ps. 27
2–Feb	Exod. 15–16	Matt. 19:1–15	Ps. 28
3–Feb	Exod. 17–19	Matt. 19:16–30	Ps. 29
4–Feb	Exod. 20–21	Matt. 20:1–19	Ps. 30
5–Feb	Exod. 22–23	Matt. 20:20–34	Ps. 31:1–8
6–Feb	Exod. 24–25	Matt. 21:1–27	Ps. 31:9–18
7–Feb	Exod 26–27	Matt. 21:28–46	Ps. 31:19–24
8–Feb	Exod. 28	Matt. 22	Ps. 32
9–Feb	Exod. 29	Matt. 23:1–36	Ps. 33:1–12
10–Feb	Exod. 30–31	Matt. 23:37–24:28	Ps. 33:13–22
11–Feb	Exod. 32–33	Matt. 24:29–51	Ps. 34:1–7
12–Feb	Exod. 34:1–35:29	Matt. 25:1–13	Ps. 34:8–22
13–Feb	Exod. 35:30–37:29	Matt. 25:14–30	Ps. 35:1–8
14–Feb	Exod. 38–39	Matt. 25:31–46	Ps. 35:9–17
15–Feb	Exod. 40	Matt. 26:1–35	Ps. 35:18–28
16–Feb	Lev. 1–3	Matt. 26:36–68	Ps. 36:1–6
17–Feb	Lev. 4:1–5:13	Matt. 26:69–27:26	Ps. 36:7–12
18–Feb	Lev. 5:14 –7:21	Matt. 27:27–50	Ps. 37:1–6
19–Feb	Lev. 7:22–8:36	Matt. 27:51–66	Ps. 37:7–26
20–Feb	Lev. 9–10	Matt. 28	Ps. 37:27–40
21–Feb	Lev. 11–12	Mark 1:1–28	Ps. 38
22–Feb	Lev. 13	Mark 1:29–39	Ps. 39
23–Feb	Lev. 14	Mark 1:40–2:12	Ps. 40:1–8
24–Feb	Lev. 15	Mark 2:13–3:35	Ps. 40:9–17
25–Feb	Lev. 16–17	Mark 4:1–20	Ps. 41:1–4
26–Feb	Lev. 18–19	Mark 4:21–41	Ps. 41:5–13
27–Feb	Lev. 20	Mark 5	Ps. 42–43

28–Feb	Lev. 21–22	Mark 6:1–13	Ps. 44
1–Mar	Lev. 23–24	Mark 6:14–29	Ps. 45:1–5
2–Mar	Lev. 25	Mark 6:30–56	Ps. 45:6–12
3–Mar	Lev. 26	Mark 7	Ps. 45:13–17
4–Mar	Lev. 27	Mark 8	Ps. 46
5–Mar	Num. 1–2	Mark 9:1–13	Ps. 47
6–Mar	Num. 3	Mark 9:14–50	Ps. 48:1–8
7–Mar	Num. 4	Mark 10:1–34	Ps. 48:9–14
8–Mar	Num. 5:1–6:21	Mark 10:35–52	Ps. 49:1–9
9–Mar	Num. 6:22–7:47	Mark 11	Ps. 49:10–20
10–Mar	Num. 7:48–8:4	Mark 12:1–27	Ps. 50:1–15
11–Mar	Num. 8:5–9:23	Mark 12:28–44	Ps. 50:16–23
12–Mar	Num. 10–11	Mark 13:1–8	Ps. 51:1–9
13–Mar	Num. 12–13	Mark 13:9–37	Ps. 51:10–19
14–Mar	Num. 14	Mark 14:1–31	Ps. 52
15–Mar	Num. 15	Mark 14:32–72	Ps. 53
16–Mar	Num. 16	Mark 15:1–32	Ps. 54
17–Mar	Num. 17–18	Mark 15:33–47	Ps. 55
18–Mar	Num. 19–20	Mark 16	Ps. 56:1–7
19–Mar	Num. 21:1–22:20	Luke 1:1–25	Ps. 56:8–13
20–Mar	Num. 22:21–23:30	Luke 1:26–56	Ps. 57
21–Mar	Num. 24–25	Luke 1:57–2:20	Ps. 58
22–Mar	Num. 26:1–27:11	Luke 2:21–38	Ps. 59:1–8
23–Mar	Num. 27:12–29:11	Luke 2:39–52	Ps. 59:9–17
24–Mar	Num. 29:12–30:16	Luke 3	Ps. 60:1–5
25–Mar	Num. 31	Luke 4	Ps. 60:6–12
26–Mar	Num. 32–33	Luke 5:1–16	Ps. 61
27–Mar	Num. 34–36	Luke 5:17–32	Ps. 62:1–6
28–Mar	Deut. 1:1–2:25	Luke 5:33–6:11	Ps. 62:7–12
29–Mar	Deut. 2:26–4:14	Luke 6:12–35	Ps. 63:1–5

30–Mar	Deut. 4:15–5:22	Luke 6:36–49	Ps. 63:6–11
31–Mar	Deut. 5:23–7:26	Luke 7:1–17	Ps. 64:1–5
1–Apr	Deut. 8–9	Luke 7:18–35	Ps. 64:6–10
2–Apr	Deut. 10–11	Luke 7:36–8:3	Ps. 65:1–8
3–Apr	Deut. 12–13	Luke 8:4–21	Ps. 65:9–13
4–Apr	Deut. 14:1–16:8	Luke 8:22–39	Ps. 66:1–7
5–Apr	Deut. 16:9–18:22	Luke 8:40–56	Ps. 66:8–15
6–Apr	Deut. 19:1–21:9	Luke 9:1–22	Ps. 66:16–20
7–Apr	Deut. 21:10–23:8	Luke 9:23–42	Ps. 67
8–Apr	Deut. 23:9–25:19	Luke 9:43–62	Ps. 68:1–6
9–Apr	Deut. 26:1–28:14	Luke 10:1–20	Ps. 68:7–14
10–Apr	Deut. 28:15–68	Luke 10:21–37	Ps. 68:15–19
11–Apr	Deut. 29–30	Luke 10:38–11:23	Ps. 68:20–27
12–Apr	Deut. 31:1–32:22	Luke 11:24–36	Ps. 68:28–35
13–Apr	Deut. 32:23–33:29	Luke 11:37–54	Ps. 69:1–9
14–Apr	Deut. 34–Josh. 2	Luke 12:1–15	Ps. 69:10–17
15–Apr	Josh. 3:1–5:12	Luke 12:16–40	Ps. 69:18–28
16–Apr	Josh. 5:13–7:26	Luke 12:41–48	Ps. 69:29–36
17–Apr	Josh. 8–9	Luke 12:49–59	Ps. 70
18–Apr	Josh. 10:1–11:15	Luke 13:1–21	Ps. 71:1–6
19–Apr	Josh. 11:16–13:33	Luke 13:22–35	Ps. 71:7–16
20–Apr	Josh. 14–16	Luke 14:1–15	Ps. 71:17–21
21–Apr	Josh. 17:1–19:16	Luke 14:16–35	Ps. 71:22–24
22–Apr	Josh. 19:17–21:42	Luke 15:1–10	Ps. 72:1–11
23–Apr	Josh. 21:43–22:34	Luke 15:11–32	Ps. 72:12–20
24–Apr	Josh. 23–24	Luke 16:1–18	Ps. 73:1–9
25–Apr	Judg. 1–2	Luke 16:19–17:10	Ps. 73:10–20
26–Apr	Judg. 3–4	Luke 17:11–37	Ps. 73:21–28
27–Apr	Judg. 5:1–6:24	Luke 18:1–17	Ps. 74:1–3
28–Apr	Judg. 6:25–7:25	Luke 18:18–43	Ps. 74:4–11

29–Apr	Judg. 8:1–9:23	Luke 19:1–28	Ps. 74:12–17
30–Apr	Judg. 9:24–10:18	Luke 19:29–48	Ps. 74:18–23
1–May	Judg. 11:1–12:7	Luke 20:1–26	Ps. 75:1–7
2–May	Judg. 12:8–14:20	Luke 20:27–47	Ps. 75:8–10
3–May	Judg. 15–16	Luke 21:1–19	Ps. 76:1–7
4–May	Judg. 17–18	Luke 21:20–22:6	Ps. 76:8–12
5–May	Judg. 19:1–20:23	Luke 22:7–30	Ps. 77:1–11
6–May	Judg. 20:24–21:25	Luke 22:31–54	Ps. 77:12–20
7–May	Ruth 1–2	Luke 22:55–23:25	Ps. 78:1–4
8–May	Ruth 3–4	Luke 23:26–24:12	Ps. 78:5–8
9–May	1 Sam. 1:1–2:21	Luke 24:13–53	Ps. 78:9–16
10–May	1 Sam. 2:22–4:22	John 1:1–28	Ps. 78:17–24
11–May	1 Sam. 5–7	John 1:29–51	Ps. 78:25–33
12–May	1 Sam. 8:1–9:26	John 2	Ps. 78:34–41
13–May	1 Sam. 9:27–11:15	John 3:1–22	Ps. 78:42–55
14–May	1 Sam. 12–13	John 3:23–4:10	Ps. 78:56–66
15–May	1 Sam. 14	John 4:11–38	Ps. 78:67–72
16–May	1 Sam. 15–16	John 4:39–54	Ps. 79:1–7
17–May	1 Sam. 17	John 5:1–24	Ps. 79:8–13
18–May	1 Sam. 18–19	John 5:25–47	Ps. 80:1–7
19–May	1 Sam. 20–21	John 6:1–21	Ps. 80:8–19
20–May	1 Sam. 22–23	John 6:22–42	Ps. 81:1–10
21–May	1 Sam. 24:1–25:31	John 6:43–71	Ps. 81:11–16
22–May	1 Sam. 25:32–27:12	John 7:1–24	Ps. 82
23–May	1 Sam. 28–29	John 7:25–8:11	Ps. 83
24–May	1 Sam. 30–31	John 8:12–47	Ps. 84:1–4
25–May	2 Sam. 1–2	John 8:48–9:12	Ps. 84:5–12
26–May	2 Sam. 3–4	John 9:13–34	Ps. 85:1–7
27–May	2 Sam. 5:1–7:17	John 9:35–10:10	Ps. 85:8–13
28–May	2 Sam. 7:18–10:19	John 10:11–30	Ps. 86:1–10

29–May	2 Sam. 11:1–12:25	John 10:31–11:16	Ps. 86:11–17
30–May	2 Sam. 12:26–13:39	John 11:17–54	Ps. 87
31–May	2 Sam. 14:1–15:12	John 11:55–12:19	Ps. 88:1–9
1–Jun	2 Sam. 15:13–16:23	John 12:20–43	Ps. 88:10–18
2–Jun	2 Sam. 17:1–18:18	John 12:44–13:20	Ps. 89:1–6
3–Jun	2 Sam. 18:19–19:39	John 13:21–38	Ps. 89:7–13
4–Jun	2 Sam. 19:40–21:22	John 14:1–17	Ps. 89:14–18
5–Jun	2 Sam. 22:1–23:7	John 14:18–15:27	Ps. 89:19–29
6–Jun	2 Sam. 23:8–24:25	John 16:1–22	Ps. 89:30–37
7–Jun	1 Kings 1	John 16:23–17:5	Ps. 89:38–52
8–Jun	1 Kings 2	John 17:6–26	Ps. 90:1–12
9–Jun	1 Kings 3–4	John 18:1–27	Ps. 90:13–17
10–Jun	1 Kings 5–6	John 18:28–19:5	Ps. 91:1–10
11–Jun	1 Kings 7	John 19:6–25a	Ps. 91:11–16
12–Jun	1 Kings 8:1–53	John 19:25b–42	Ps. 92:1–9
13–Jun	1 Kings 8:54–10:13	John 20:1–18	Ps. 92:10–15
14–Jun	1 Kings 10:14–11:43	John 20:19–31	Ps. 93
15–Jun	1 Kings 12:1–13:10	John 21	Ps. 94:1–11
16–Jun	1 Kings 13:11–14:31	Acts 1:1–11	Ps. 94:12–23
17–Jun	1 Kings 15:1–16:20	Acts 1:12–26	Ps. 95
18–Jun	1 Kings 16:21–18:19	Acts 2:1–21	Ps. 96:1–8
19–Jun	1 Kings 18:20–19:21	Acts 2:22–41	Ps. 96:9–13
20–Jun	1 Kings 20	Acts 2:42–3:26	Ps. 97:1–6
21–Jun	1 Kings 21:1–22:28	Acts 4:1–22	Ps. 97:7–12
22–Jun	1 Kings 22:29– 2 Kings 1:18	Acts 4:23–5:11	Ps. 98
23–Jun	2 Kings 2–3	Acts 5:12–28	Ps. 99
24–Jun	2 Kings 4	Acts 5:29–6:15	Ps. 100
25–Jun	2 Kings 5:1–6:23	Acts 7:1–16	Ps. 101
26–Jun	2 Kings 6:24–8:15	Acts 7:17–36	Ps. 102:1–7

27–Jun	2 Kings 8:16–9:37	Acts 7:37–53	Ps. 102:8–17
28–Jun	2 Kings 10–11	Acts 7:54–8:8	Ps. 102:18–28
29–Jun	2 Kings 12–13	Acts 8:9–40	Ps. 103:1–9
30–Jun	2 Kings 14–15	Acts 9:1–16	Ps. 103:10–14
1–Jul	2 Kings 16–17	Acts 9:17–31	Ps. 103:15–22
2–Jul	2 Kings 18:1–19:7	Acts 9:32–10:16	Ps. 104:1–9
3–Jul	2 Kings 19:8–20:21	Acts 10:17–33	Ps. 104:10–23
4–Jul	2 Kings 21:1–22:20	Acts 10:34–11:18	Ps. 104: 24–30
5–Jul	2 Kings 23	Acts 11:19–12:17	Ps. 104:31–35
6–Jul	2 Kings 24–25	Acts 12:18–13:13	Ps. 105:1–7
7–Jul	1 Chron. 1–2	Acts 13:14–43	Ps. 105:8–15
8–Jul	1 Chron. 3:1–5:10	Acts 13:44–14:10	Ps. 105:16–28
9–Jul	1 Chron. 5:11–6:81	Acts 14:11–28	Ps. 105:29–36
10–Jul	1 Chron. 7:1–9:9	Acts 15:1–18	Ps. 105:37–45
11–Jul	1 Chron. 9:10–11:9	Acts 15:19–41	Ps. 106:1–12
12–Jul	1 Chron. 11:10–12:40	Acts 16:1–15	Ps. 106:13–27
13–Jul	1 Chron. 13–15	Acts 16:16–40	Ps. 106:28–33
14–Jul	1 Chron. 16–17	Acts 17:1–14	Ps. 106:34–43
15–Jul	1 Chron. 18–20	Acts 17:15–34	Ps. 106:44–48
16–Jul	1 Chron. 21–22	Acts 18:1–23	Ps. 107:1–9
17–Jul	1 Chron. 23–25	Acts 18:24–19:10	Ps. 107:10–16
18–Jul	1 Chron. 26–27	Acts 19:11–22	Ps. 107:17–32
19–Jul	1 Chron. 28–29	Acts 19:23–41	Ps. 107:33–38
20–Jul	2 Chron. 1–3	Acts 20:1–16	Ps. 107:39–43
21–Jul	2 Chron. 4:1–6:11	Acts 20:17–38	Ps. 108
22–Jul	2 Chron. 6:12–7:10	Acts 21:1–14	Ps. 109:1–20
23–Jul	2 Chron. 7:11–9:28	Acts 21:15–32	Ps. 109:21–31
24–Jul	2 Chron. 9:29–12:16	Acts 21:33–22:16	Ps. 110:1–3
25–Jul	2 Chron. 13–15	Acts 22:17–23:11	Ps. 110:4–7
26–Jul	2 Chron. 16–17	Acts 23:12–24:21	Ps. 111

27–Jul	2 Chron. 18–19	Acts 24:22–25:12	Ps. 112
28–Jul	2 Chron. 20–21	Acts 25:13–27	Ps. 113
29–Jul	2 Chron. 22–23	Acts 26	Ps. 114
30–Jul	2 Chron. 24:1–25:16	Acts 27:1–20	Ps. 115:1–10
31–Jul	2 Chron. 25:17–27:9	Acts 27:21–28:6	Ps. 115:11–18
1–Aug	2 Chron. 28:1–29:19	Acts 28:7–31	Ps. 116:1–5
2–Aug	2 Chron. 29:20–30:27	Rom. 1:1–17	Ps. 116:6–19
3–Aug	2 Chron. 31–32	Rom. 1:18–32	Ps. 117
4–Aug	2 Chron. 33:1–34:7	Rom. 2	Ps. 118:1–18
5–Aug	2 Chron. 34:8–35:19	Rom. 3:1–26	Ps. 118:19–23
6–Aug	2 Chron. 35:20–36:23	Rom. 3:27–4:25	Ps. 118:24–29
7–Aug	Ezra 1–3	Rom. 5	Ps. 119:1–8
8–Aug	Ezra 4–5	Rom. 6:1–7:6	Ps. 119:9–16
9–Aug	Ezra 6:1–7:26	Rom. 7:7–25	Ps. 119:17–32
10–Aug	Ezra 7:27–9:4	Rom. 8:1–27	Ps. 119:33–40
11–Aug	Ezra 9:5–10:44	Rom. 8:28–39	Ps. 119:41–64
12–Aug	Neh. 1:1–3:16	Rom. 9:1–18	Ps. 119:65–72
13–Aug	Neh. 3:17–5:13	Rom. 9:19–33	Ps. 119:73–80
14–Aug	Neh. 5:14–7:73	Rom. 10:1–13	Ps. 119:81–88
15–Aug	Neh. 8:1–9:5	Rom. 10:14–11:24	Ps. 119:89–104
16–Aug	Neh. 9:6–10:27	Rom. 11:25–12:8	Ps. 119:105–120
17–Aug	Neh. 10:28–12:26	Rom. 12:9–13:7	Ps. 119:121–128
18–Aug	Neh. 12:27–13:31	Rom. 13:8–14:12	Ps. 119:129–136
19–Aug	Esther 1:1–2:18	Rom. 14:13–15:13	Ps. 119:137–152
20–Aug	Esther 2:19–5:14	Rom. 15:14–21	Ps. 119:153–168
21–Aug	Esther. 6–8	Rom. 15:22–33	Ps. 119:169–176
22–Aug	Esther 9–10	Rom. 16	Ps. 120–122
23–Aug	Job 1–3	1 Cor. 1:1–25	Ps. 123
24–Aug	Job 4–6	1 Cor. 1:26–2:16	Ps. 124–125
25–Aug	Job 7–9	1 Cor. 3	Ps. 126–127

26–Aug	Job 10–13	1 Cor. 4:1–13	Ps. 128–129
27–Aug	Job 14–16	1 Cor. 4:14–5:13	Ps. 130
28–Aug	Job 17–20	1 Cor. 6	Ps. 131
29–Aug	Job 21–23	1 Cor. 7:1–16	Ps. 132
30–Aug	Job 24–27	1 Cor. 7:17–40	Ps. 133–134
31–Aug	Job 28–30	1 Cor. 8	Ps. 135
1–Sep	Job 31–33	1 Cor. 9:1–18	Ps. 136:1–9
2–Sep	Job 34–36	1 Cor. 9:19–10:13	Ps. 136:10–26
3–Sep	Job 37–39	1 Cor. 10:14–11:1	Ps. 137
4–Sep	Job 40–42	1 Cor. 11:2–34	Ps. 138
5–Sep	Eccles. 1:1–3:15	1 Cor. 12:1–26	Ps. 139:1–6
6–Sep	Eccles. 3:16–6:12	1 Cor. 12:27–13:13	Ps. 139:7–18
7–Sep	Eccles. 7:1–9:12	1 Cor. 14:1–22	Ps. 139:19–24
8–Sep	Eccles. 9:13–12:14	1 Cor. 14:23–15:11	Ps. 140:1–8
9–Sep	SS 1–4	1 Cor. 15:12–34	Ps. 140:9–13
10–Sep	SS 5–8	1 Cor. 15:35–58	Ps. 141
11–Sep	Isa. 1–2	1 Cor. 16	Ps. 142
12–Sep	Isa. 3–5	2 Cor. 1:1–11	Ps. 143:1–6
13–Sep	Isa. 6–8	2 Cor. 1:12–2:4	Ps. 143:7–12
14–Sep	Isa. 9–10	2 Cor. 2:5–17	Ps. 144
15–Sep	Isa. 11–13	2 Cor. 3	Ps. 145
16–Sep	Isa. 14–16	2 Cor. 4	Ps. 146
17–Sep	Isa. 17–19	2 Cor. 5	Ps. 147:1–11
18–Sep	Isa. 20–23	2 Cor. 6	Ps. 147:12–20
19–Sep	Isa. 24:1–26:19	2 Cor. 7	Ps. 148
20–Sep	Isa. 26:20–28:29	2 Cor. 8	Ps. 149–150
21 Sep	Isa. 29–30	2 Cor. 9	Prov. 1:1–9
22–Sep	Isa. 31–33	2 Cor. 10	Prov. 1:10–22
23–Sep	Isa. 34–36	2 Cor. 11	Prov. 1:23–26
24–Sep	Isa. 37–38	2 Cor. 12:1–10	Prov. 1:27–33

25–Sep	Isa. 39–40	2 Cor. 12:11–13:14	Prov. 2:1–15
26–Sep	Isa. 41–42	Gal. 1	Prov. 2:16–22
27–Sep	Isa. 43:1–44:20	Gal. 2	Prov. 3:1–12
28–Sep	Isa. 44:21–46:13	Gal. 3:1–18	Prov. 3:13–26
29–Sep	Isa. 47:1–49:13	Gal 3:19–29	Prov. 3:27–35
30–Sep	Isa. 49:14–51:23	Gal 4:1–11	Prov. 4:1–19
1–Oct	Isa. 52–54	Gal. 4:12–31	Prov. 4:20–27
2–Oct	Isa. 55–57	Gal. 5	Prov. 5:1–14
3–Oct	Isa. 58–59	Gal. 6	Prov. 5:15–23
4–Oct	Isa. 60–62	Eph. 1	Prov. 6:1–5
5–Oct	Isa. 63:1–65:16	Eph. 2	Prov. 6:6–19
6–Oct	Isa. 65:17–66:24	Eph. 3:1–4:16	Prov. 6:20–26
7–Oct	Jer. 1–2	Eph. 4:17–32	Prov. 6:27–35
8–Oct	Jer. 3:1–4:22	Eph. 5	Prov. 7:1–5
9–Oct	Jer. 4:23–5:31	Eph. 6	Prov. 7:6–27
10–Oct	Jer. 6:1–7:26	Phil. 1:1–26	Prov. 8:1–11
11–Oct	Jer. 7:26–9:16	Phil. 1:27–2:18	Prov. 8:12–21
12–Oct	Jer. 9:17–11:17	Phil 2:19–30	Prov. 8:22–36
13–Oct	Jer. 11:18–13:27	Phil. 3	Prov. 9:1–6
14–Oct	Jer. 14–15	Phil. 4	Prov. 9:7–18
15–Oct	Jer. 16–17	Col. 1:1–23	Prov. 10:1–5
16–Oct	Jer. 18:1–20:6	Col. 1:24–2:15	Prov. 10:6–14
17–Oct	Jer. 20:7–22:19	Col. 2:16–3:4	Prov. 10:15–26
18–Oct	Jer. 22:20–23:40	Col. 3:5–4:1	Prov. 10:27–32
19–Oct	Jer. 24–25	Col. 4:2–18	Prov. 11:1–11
20–Oct	Jer. 26–27	1 Thes. 1:1–2:8	Prov. 11:12–21
21–Oct	Jer. 28–29	1 Thes. 2:9–3:13	Prov. 11:22–26
22–Oct	Jer. 30:1–31:22	1 Thes. 4:1–5:11	Prov. 11:27–31
23–Oct	Jer. 31:23–32:35	1 Thes. 5:12–28	Prov. 12:1–14
24–Oct	Jer. 32:36–34:7	2 Thes. 1–2	Prov. 12:15–20

25–Oct	Jer. 34:8–36:10	2 Thes. 3	Prov. 12:21–28
26–Oct	Jer. 36:11–38:13	1 Tim. 1:1–17	Prov. 13:1–4
27–Oct	Jer. 38:14–40:6	1 Tim. 1:18–3:13	Prov. 13:5–13
28–Oct	Jer. 40:7–42:22	1 Tim. 3:14–4:10	Prov. 13:14–21
29–Oct	Jer. 43–44	1 Tim. 4:11–5:16	Prov. 13:22–25
30–Oct	Jer. 45–47	1 Tim. 5:17–6:21	Prov. 14:1–6
31–Oct	Jer. 48:1–49:6	2 Tim. 1	Prov. 14:7–22
1–Nov	Jer. 49:7–50:16	2 Tim. 2	Prov. 14:23–27
2–Nov	Jer. 50:17–51:14	2 Tim. 3	Prov. 14:28–35
3–Nov	Jer. 51:15–64	2 Tim. 4	Prov. 15:1–9
4–Nov	Jer. 52–Lam. 1	Ti. 1:1–9	Prov. 15:10–17
5–Nov	Lam. 2:1–3:38	Ti. 1:10–2:15	Prov. 15:18–26
6–Nov	Lam. 3:39 5:22	Ti. 3	Prov. 15.27–33
7–Nov	Ezek. 1:1–3:21	Philemon 1	Prov. 16:1–9
8–Nov	Ezek. 3:22–5:17	Heb. 1:1–2:4	Prov. 16:10–21
9–Nov	Ezek. 6–7	Heb. 2:5–18	Prov. 16:22–33
10–Nov	Ezek. 8–10	Heb. 3:1–4:3	Prov. 17:1–5
11–Nov	Ezek. 11–12	Heb. 4:4–5:10	Prov. 17:6–12
12–Nov	Ezek. 13–14	Heb. 5:11–6:20	Prov. 17:13–22
13–Nov	Ezek. 15:1–16:43	Heb. 7:1–28	Prov. 17:23–28
14–Nov	Ezek. 16:44–17:24	Heb. 8:1–9:10	Prov. 18:1–7
15–Nov	Ezek. 18–19	Heb. 9:11–28	Prov. 18:8–17
16–Nov	Ezek. 20	Heb. 10:1–25	Prov. 18:18–24
17–Nov	Ezek. 21–22	Heb. 10:26–39	Prov. 19:1–8
18–Nov	Ezek. 23	Heb. 11:1–31	Prov. 19:9–14
19–Nov	Ezek. 24–26	Heb. 11:32–40	Prov. 19:15–21
20–Nov	Ezek. 27–28	Heb. 12:1–13	Prov. 19:22–29
21–Nov	Ezek. 29–30	Heb. 12:14–29	Prov. 20:1–18
22–Nov	Ezek. 31–32	Heb. 13	Prov. 20:19–24
23–Nov	Ezek. 33:1–34:10	Jas. 1	Prov. 20:25–30

Notes

Notes

Notes

Notes

About the Author

Rae Simons is the pen name of a gifted inspirational romance author from New York. Rae has spent several years editing and proofreading the work of other authors, and in 1995 she proved that she has what it takes to write her own novels when *The Quiet Heart* debuted with Heartsong.